PLEBS
ROMANA

PLEBS ROMANA

People, Power
and Politics in
Ancient Rome

PETER JONES

Atlantic Books
London

First published in hardback in Great Britain in 2025 by Atlantic Books,
an imprint of Atlantic Books Ltd.

Map artwork by Jeff Edwards.

10 9 8 7 6 5 4 3 2

A CIP catalogue record for this book is available from the British Library.

Hardback ISBN: 978 1 80546 510 2
E-book ISBN: 978 1 80546 511 9

Design by Carrdesignstudio.com
Printed and bound by CPI (UK) Ltd, Croydon CR0 4YY

Atlantic Books
An imprint of Atlantic Books Ltd
Ormond House
26–27 Boswell Street
London
WC1N 3JZ

www.atlantic-books.co.uk

Product safety EU representative: Authorised Rep Compliance Ltd.,
Ground Floor, 71 Lower Baggot Street, Dublin, D02 P593, Ireland.
www.arccompliance.com

MIX
Paper | Supporting
responsible forestry
FSC
www.fsc.org
FSC® C013604

The book is dedicated to Lindsay and our family, sine quibus non: *Philippa (White), Phoebe, Tom and Jill (Hurworth), and Paul (White), Charlotte, Toby and Helena.*

CONTENTS

MAPS

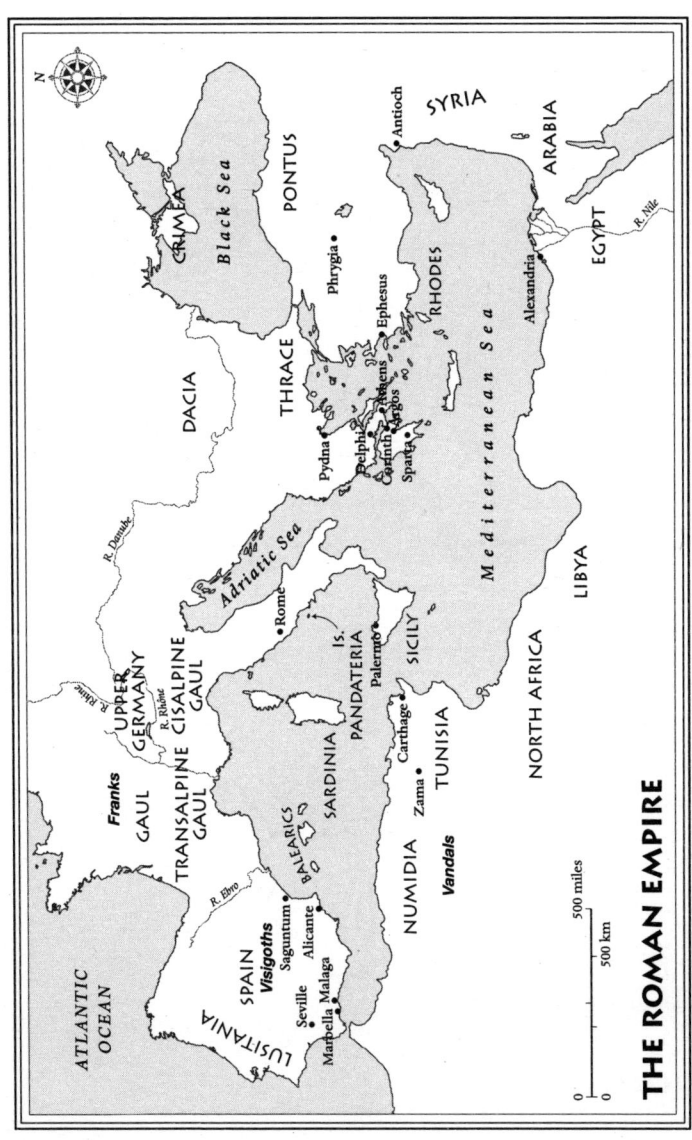

THE ROMAN EMPIRE

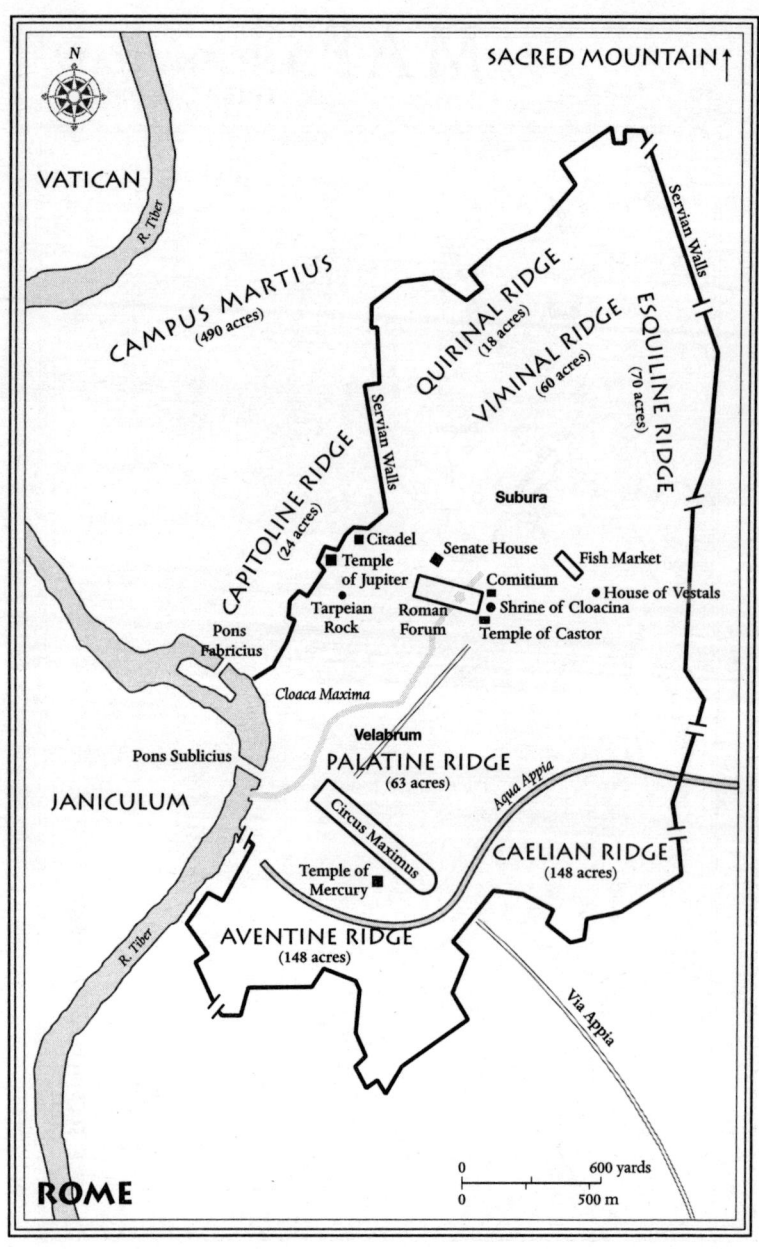

N

SACRED MOUNTAIN↑

VATICAN

R. Tiber

CAMPUS MARTIUS
(490 acres)

QUIRINAL RIDGE
(18 acres)

VIMINAL RIDGE
(60 acres)

ESQUILINE RIDGE
(70 acres)

Servian Walls

CAPITOLINE RIDGE
(24 acres)

Servian Walls

Subura

■ Citadel

■ Temple
of Jupiter

■ Tarpeian
Rock

◆ Senate House

Comitium

Roman
Forum

◆ Shrine of Cloacina

■ Temple of Castor

☐ Fish Market

● House of Vestals

Pons
Fabricius

Cloaca Maxima

Pons Sublicius

JANICULUM

Velabrum

PALATINE RIDGE
(63 acres)

Aqua Appia

CAELIAN RIDGE
(148 acres)

Circus Maximus

Temple of
Mercury ■

AVENTINE RIDGE
(148 acres)

Via Appia

R. Tiber

ROME

0   600 yards

0   500 m

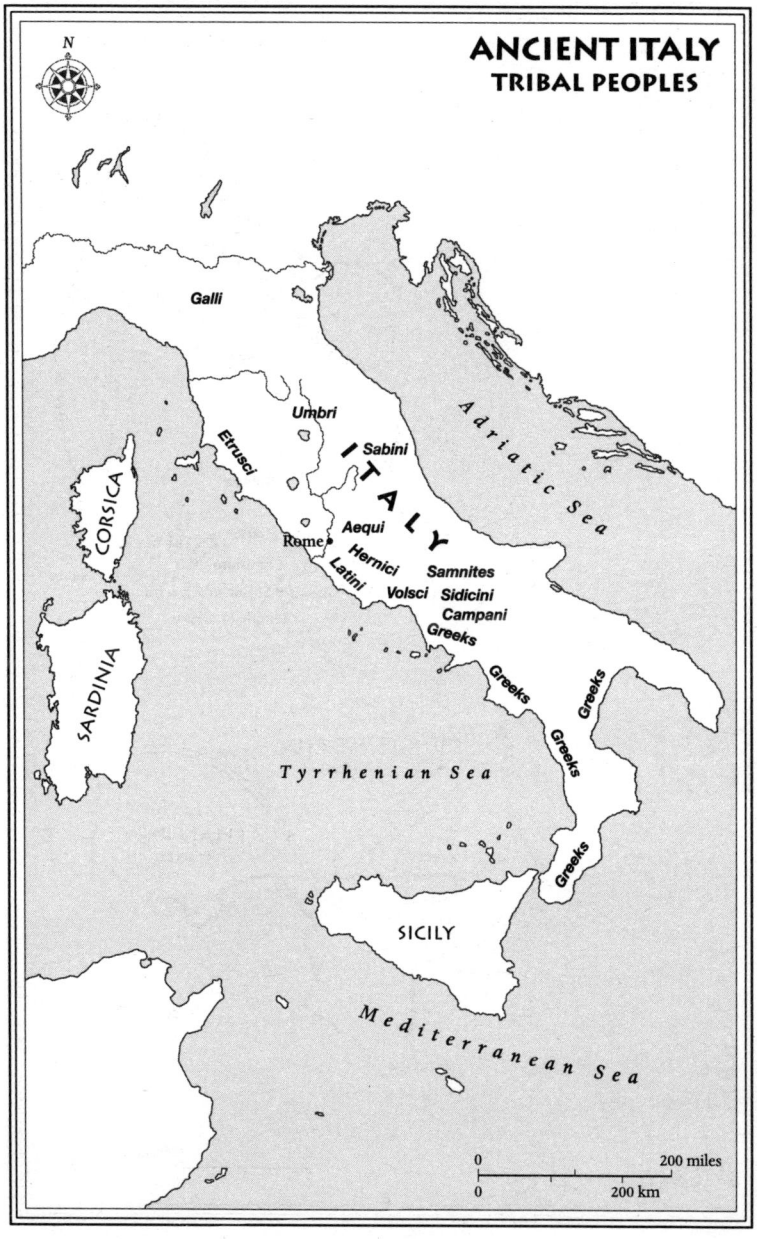

ANCIENT ITALY
TRIBAL PEOPLES

N

Galli

Umbri

Etrusci

Sabini

A d r i a t i c   S e a

I T A L Y

CORSICA

Aequi

Rome

Hernici

Samnites

Latini

Volsci *Sidicini*

Campani

Greeks

SARDINIA

T y r r h e n i a n   S e a

Greeks

Greeks

Greeks

SICILY

M e d i t e r r a n e a n   S e a

0		200 miles
0		200 km

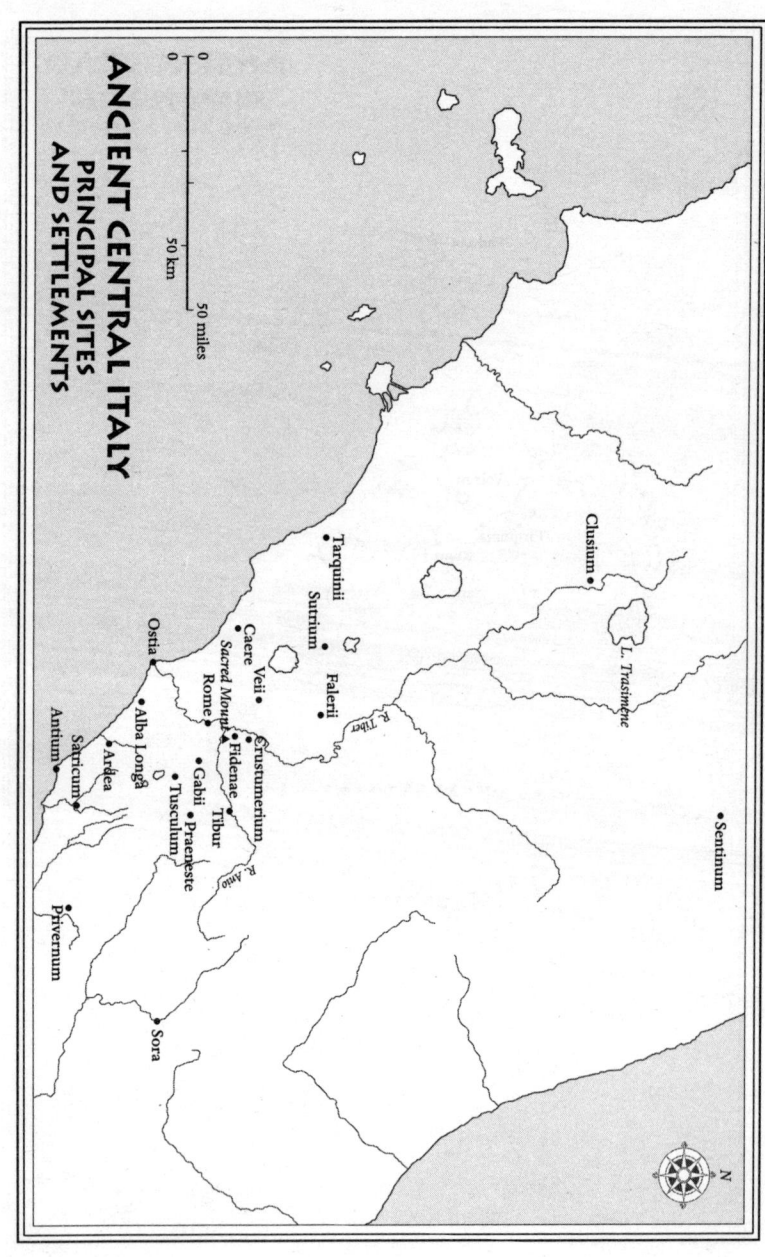

ANCIENT CENTRAL ITALY
PRINCIPAL SITES
AND SETTLEMENTS

0
0
50 km
50 miles

Tarquinii
Surrium
Caere
Veii
Faleri
Ostia
Sacred Mount
Rome
Crustumerium
Fidenae
Alba Longa
Gabii
Tibur
Antium
Satricum
Praeneste
Ardea
Tusculum
Privernum
Sora
Clusium
L. Trasimene
Sentinum
R. Tiber
R. Anio

N

ANCIENT ITALY
PRINCIPAL SITES
AND SETTLEMENTS

N

Nola
Naples
Cumae
Puteoli   Pompei
Nuceria

Padua

Adriatic Sea

ITALY

CORSICA

Volsini
Tarquinia   Veii
Rome Gabii
Satricum   *V. Appia*
Capua   *Caudine Forks* Venusia
Tarentum
Heraclea

SARDINIA

Tyrrhenian Sea

MAGNA GRAECIA

Messina

SICILY

Carthage

Mediterranean Sea

0   200 miles
0   200 km

FOREWORD

If you were among the richest half a per cent of the Roman population, you might think that the world owed you a living. All other free Romans – the *plebs* – knew that the world did not. For the poor among them, simple survival was the bottom line.

There were four constants:

Nearly 90 per cent of Romans were peasant farmers, living off what their farm could produce. A bad harvest could be the end of them. Most of the remaining 10 per cent were city dwellers, e.g. artisans, labourers, etc. The remaining minority were the extremely wealthy elite. Slaves, of course, did not count as Romans. They made up about 10 per cent of the total population, nearer 20 per cent in the cities.

The welfare state did not exist. Only a famine would cause the state to step in, at least for those living in the city.

Of children born, half would be dead by the age of five. Only one in three of those would make it to forty.

The best that most *plebs* could hope for – though some were wealthy – was a degree of security. That began with the family but extended to friends and, more widely, the local community. It was up to you to ensure your relationships with those three groupings were productive. If they weren't, you were in serious trouble.

The Greek peasant poet-farmer Hesiod (d. c. 680 BC, contemporary with early Rome), gave a picture of the peasant farmer's priorities. In his poem 'Works and Days', he sees farming as a matter of survival, when men 'will never cease from toil and misery by day and night'.

His advice makes clear what is needed to succeed. 'Do not put things off till tomorrow and the next day. That man never fills his granary. It is application that produces increase. The man who puts off work wrestles with ruin.'

Look after what you produce, he recommends: 'If you lay down even a little on a little, and do this often, that could well grow big; he who adds to what is there keeps hunger at bay.' Protect what you have: 'What is stored away at home is never a worry; better to have things there in the house than outside.'

The consequences could be dramatic: 'It is through work that men become rich in flocks and wealthy, and a working man is much dearer to the immortals. Work is no disgrace, but idleness is; and if you work, you will soon find the idle man will envy you as you enrich yourself – for wealth is accompanied by honour and prestige.' The sentiment is very Greek: nothing beats people looking up to you.

There was a degree of community cooperation in all this: 'It is good to take a measure from your neighbour and good to pay him back the same, or better, so that if you are in need afterwards, you can rely on him for help.'

But there was also a strong sense of competition: 'A man is keen to work when he sees his rich neighbour ploughing and planting and putting his house in order, and neighbour vies with neighbour as he hurries after wealth... potter competes with potter, and craftsman with craftsman.'

That world was not going to change. No one ever thought it could, or would, or even should. But one could always hope for a slice of luck – and for that one had better keep men and gods on side.

THE OTHER SIDE OF THIS STORY

But when it came to politics and rich people telling you what to do in *their* interests and not in yours… that was a very different matter altogether. It is no coincidence that that one of the most regularly repeated aphorisms in the ancient world was 'do good to your friends and harm to your enemies'.

The subject of this book – and it is an eye-opener – is the Romans' story of how the *plebs*, over some 700 years from Rome's foundation in 753 BC, managed to turn themselves into a significant body in opposition to the elite, changing the whole political landscape, and in the process acting as the driving force that resulted in Rome becoming the master of Italy and beginning a gradual expansion into North Africa, Gaul, much of the Mediterranean, and the Greek and Near Eastern worlds.

But what happened next? On the one hand, civil war and the end of the republic in 27 BC; on the other, 450 years of rule by emperors – even a *pleb* could become an emperor – and an even larger empire that finally collapsed in AD 476. It is fair to say that if the *plebs* had not achieved what they did in reforming the relationship between rich and poor during the republican period, chipping away at elite structures and gradually carving out influence for themselves, it is most unlikely that any of this could have happened. And the consequences for *our* political world have been dramatic.

This story, up to the end of the republic, will be the one told by the Roman historian Livy. Selecting the most significant incidents and moments from his surviving Roman history, we shall follow closely the ups and downs of the *plebs'* many battles for political power, in a way that I am not aware has ever been done before, and end with a general assessment of the place of the *plebs* in the new world that emerged under the emperor Augustus (27 BC–AD 14), with a particular focus on Pompeii.

INTRODUCTION

PLEBS AND PATRICIANS

In the ancient Roman world, the word *plebs* referred to *one* of the three social categories into which that world was divided.

- The top category was 'patrician', which referred to those elite males originally selected by Romulus to be his advisory body. Over the years this grew into the 600-man-strong Senate.

- The second category was the *plebs*, i.e. *every other* free Roman. This covered everyone from the rich through to a poor peasant farmer scraping a living as best he could, or a labourer always looking for work, or a down-and-out begging in the street.

- The third category was made up of the unfree, i.e. slaves.

THE NATURAL WORLD

The only resource the ancient world had (except for humans) was *nature*, and men could tamper with or exploit it only in very limited ways, e.g. by heating, sawing, mixing, using sails, and so on.

Nature being the sole resource, everyone wanted to get as much control over it as possible. That meant conquering and holding territory, and its human, animal and mineral components. The more you had of that, the richer and more powerful you were – and you were therefore in a better position both to defend your territory against others and to expand it by conquering others.

It was, then, a 'dog eats dog' world, where everyone was fighting to maintain what they had of the natural world and trying to get more of it. And who did the fighting? Why, the males among the free Roman population, i.e. the *plebs*, most of them farmers.

THE CITY-STATE

Rome was a form of city-state. That is, Rome was a free, independent city, and the state consisted of Rome with its surrounding countryside and its people who saw Rome as their political home. That form of relationship between town and country was typical across the Greek and Roman world.

THE FARMER'S LIFE

The long, hot, dry Mediterranean summers do not represent ideal growing conditions. The farmer well understood that the more diverse his crops, the fewer the risks. The sowing and harvesting of crops therefore went on for much of the year. Grain was *the* staple crop, and grapes and olives (longer in coming to fruition) were very common.

Winter was a time of relaxation, and March welcomed in the new agricultural year. The farmer's life was not made any easier by the fact that summer was also the time for fighting, when he could be on the battle line much of the time.

This could mean big set pieces, or local raids, during which armies ravaged the countryside around rival cities where their farmer-*plebs* lived, burned down farm buildings and villages, cut down fruit trees, left no corn standing, seized cattle, and took off as slaves all the men they could lay their hands on, before the fight-back.

OLIVE OIL

One study suggests that Romans consumed something between twenty-five and fifty litres of olive oil every year. It was used for the most part as an ingredient for flavouring rather than for cooking. But it had many other purposes. The oil lamp was the main form of illumination in the home (one litre has been shown to last about 130 hours). It was also used as a moisturizing oil, a cleansing agent and the base for perfumes and cosmetics, as well as in medical treatments, the treatment of textiles and wool, and for lubrication. It was used as a contraceptive, as was cedar oil. After pressing, the solid residue could be a fuel, animal feed or fertilizer; the liquid residue, black and sticky, functioned as a fertilizer, moth repellent, insecticide, wood preserver, skin cure, waterproofer and animal tonic.

LANDOWNERS AND TENANTS

Poor *plebs* lived off the land as tenant-farmers. Those who actually *owned* that land – the wealthy elite among the patricians and *plebs* – clearly had an interest in protecting their investment, as did their tenants in being protected.

Whatever the army was like in Romulus' time (eighth century BC), it was up to the landowner to see that his tenants and retainers were given the necessary training and equipment to ensure they were capable of defending their land in the case of attack. The vast majority of *plebs* had to fight as well as farm.

That was in the interests of both sides of the social divide: the wealthy on the one hand, the *plebs* on the other. The two groups *needed* each other. In those very early years, war was probably something like a protracted scrap between about 100 men or so, for precious resources. But that would change as Rome grew over the next 150 years.

THE RIGHT RECRUITS

The military writer Vegetius (c. AD 430) said that it was not the city dwellers but countrymen that the army needed. 'They live under the open sky in a life of work, enduring the sun, not caring about shade, ignorant of bath-houses or luxury, simple people, content with little, limbs hardened to endure every type of labour, and used to wielding iron tools, digging a ditch or carrying a load.'

PEASANT – OR VNP(L)EASANT – LIFE

The following unique account of a poor *pleb*'s morning was composed by an unnamed poet c. AD 15. He describes how one Simylus started his day – as close to the life of a *pleb* living on the edge of survival as one can get. Simylus begins by making his breakfast – *moretum*, a common and simple meal often prepared with cheese and aromatic herbs, fresh or dried, many not well known by name to most of us.

The early-morning bird sang out the day and, as the light grew, Simylus, farmer of a tiny acre and fearing hunger, let himself down from his cheap bed, and feeling about in the dark for the hearth finally finds it – ouch! A little smoke still hung around a burnt log, ash covering living coals.

He bends down and lights his lamp, draws out the wick with a needle, and puffs rapidly at it to awaken the flame. *[He must keep a fire burning all the time if he wants light and heat. Otherwise, he will have to fetch a light from a neighbour.]*

At last, it catches and, shielding the flame from the draught with a hand *[his dwelling is not wind proof]*, he opens the door of his storeroom with a key. There on the ground was a poor heap of corn. *[Grain is precious: it must be secured against hard times.]*

He takes as much as he needs, sits by his hand-mill, puts the light on a board fixed to the wall, frees both arms and uses the tail of the goatskin around him to brush the headstone and the lapstone clean. *[He is about to grind the corn to produce flour.]* The left hand feeds in the grain, the right does the work. He spins the wheel and keeps it whirling, and the ground corn pours out.

AGRICULTURAL GODS

Farming was very hard work, and farmers needed all the help they could get. But there were plenty of gods to help: *Runcina,* goddess of weeding; *Robigo,* protector against mildew and rust; *Vervactor,* god of ploughing; *Stercus,* god of muck spreading; *Insitor,* god of planting seed; *Occator,* god of harrows; *Serritor,* god of digging; *Messor,* god of reaping; *Conditor,* god of storing grain.

Now he shouts to Scybale, his only housekeeper. She's African. Her whole person tells her nation – tight-curled hair, lips swollen, swarthy looks, broad chest, limp-hanging breasts, and narrow belly, thin in the legs and large feet, her torn shoes stiff and cracking everywhere. *[Is she his slave? His concubine? She certainly shares the work – two of the poor, in need of and supporting each other.]* He calls her to put dry wood on the hearth to heat up the water.

When he has ground the right amount, he pours the flour into a sieve and shakes it, leaving the husks on the top while the flour sinks down through the small holes. On a smooth board, he pours warmish water on it, folds the flour and fluid together, and kneads it firm and solid.

He scatters the dough with salt, smooths it, spreads it around, and marks it out in equal quarters. Then on the hearth – Scybale had cleaned a place – he covers it with tiles and heaps fire on top.

While fire does its work on the dough on the hearth, Simylus does not rest but, in case plain dough does not appeal, he gets food to spice it. He had no meat-racks hung beside the hearth, no hard salt ham or bacon slices curing *[real poverty here: not even any meat]*, only a round of cheese and dill, old and tightly tied in a bundle. So our provident hero looks for more provisions.

The small house had a garden, fenced with walls of willow and reeds, small but rich in varied herbs. He had there everything a poor man needs. Sometimes a rich man, wanting more of such things, came asking.

His small estate costs nothing, only care. If heavy rain or holiday kept him home at liberty *['holiday' here refers to a festival, of which there were many in Rome]*, or if the grind of ploughing paused, he worked in the garden. He arranged his plants, and knowing the soil, knew what to sow, and could bring water in from handy streams.

Here greens were thriving, here wide-waving beets, fast-growing sorrel, elecampane and mallow, rampion and leeks, lettuce, radish growing to a point, and heavy marrow letting out its belly.

This crop's not for the master but for the townsmen – every end of week, he carries it bundled on his back to market, and returns with neck relieved, weighed down with cash, but scarcely ever with the city's goods. *[This is his market garden,*

his surplus, which he takes to market to sell for cash.] Red onions,
the chive-bed, keep his hunger down, watercress, whose sharp
bite draws in one's cheeks, endives, and rocket that recalls
desire for sex.

Thinking of this he goes out into his garden and lightly
fingering back the soil, he first brings out four garlic bulbs in
all their wrappings, then he picks frothy parsley and stiff rue
and coriander.

He gathers them up and sits by the cheerful fire and loudly
calls the girl to bring his mortar. *[He prepares to pound the
herbs into a pesto.]*

He strips the garlic heads of fibrous membrane, peels off
the skin and throws the unwanted bits around the floor. The
bulb, now free of leafage, he wets and drops into the bowl of
stone.

He sprinkles salt-grains, cheese (as the salt melts) over the
garlic, and, on top, those herbs. He props up the bowl in his
hairy groin with the left hand, in his right bruises the strongly
smelling garlic with pestle-blows, then grinds it all to juice.

The hand goes round and round; the ingredients slowly
lose their particular strength, their colours blend – not wholly
green (some milky lumps resist) nor simply milky (herbs still
speckle it).

Often the sharp smell spears his widened nostrils, with
turned-up nose he gives thumbs down to food, often wipes
watering eyes with the back of his hand and madly curses at
the innocent fume.

But his work goes on: not bumping as before, but heavier,
in slow swirls, the pestle went. So he drips in a splash of
Athena's oil *[olive oil]*, and pours on top strong vinegar, very
little, mixes it in, then works it all again.

At length he glides two fingers round the mortar and
pulls the scattered bits into one ball, a perfect sample of a real
moretum.

Attentive Scybale has dug out the bread *[that he has been
baking in the 'oven']* which he embraces warmly. Now his fear
of hunger is banished; carefree for that day, Simylus arms in
leather greaves and helmet, shoves his obedient bullocks into
their yoke-straps: drives them to field: and plunges the plough
in earth.*

Note that the hard-working peasant's aim was to be self-sufficient,
a greatly admired attribute. To achieve that, he needed some of
his produce left over to sell or exchange for the other goods and
services required for simple existence (e.g. salt, mending or buying
implements, paying rent or interest on debt).

The poet tells us that Simylus' garden served this purpose:
every week he took the surplus produce to market to make what he
could from it. At the same time, the peasant had to adopt tactics
that would see him through periods of unexpected shortage. Since
staple cereals like grain could keep for up to two years, Simylus

---

* Based on Alistair Elliot's translation published in *ad familiares* vol. X (1997).

would have had a store of grain – but locked away, so precious was it. Meat was normally far too expensive to have played any part in his diet.

THE STUFF OF LIFE

Bread was the Romans' staple food. Made with many kinds of cereals and legumes reduced to flour, it was prepared with or without yeast; sometimes milk, wine, extra-virgin olive oil, fruit juice, and other ingredients were added.

Observe that Simylus was not a loner but part of a community. A rich man might call round at any time, and there was a local market, which he attended every week. He was in fact typical of those peasants who, with various sizes of holdings, made up the great majority of the Roman population.

But it is a pleasingly idealized picture. Who knows what tomorrow would bring? Destructive weather? The death of his bullocks? Illness? An assault from the many enemies surrounding Rome?

The other real fear was famine. Mercifully, this was rare. But in such a situation, cities would simply commandeer whatever they could, leaving the peasant to the grim consequences (so ancient sources tell us) of a diet of twigs, tree-shoots, bulbs, roots and grasses.

BASIC ROMAN FOOD

The poor subsisted on the less nourishing and therefore cheaper foods, e.g. barley, dried pulses (chickpeas, lentils, dried peas and beans), fruits and greens. Emmer, a species of wheat now used for breakfast cereals and fodder, was the basis of Roman porridge, a very common food during this early period, often mixed with beans and (something of a luxury) bacon. Such a diet was actually the *basic* standard for the Romans through the ages.

THE RICH

Just to give a sense of the people we are talking about, here is a list of the *surviving* names of jobs (preserved on burial jars in which the ashes were placed) of just a few of those slaves who worked in the household of the incredibly wealthy Statilius family in Rome (first century BC) over a period of about sixty years: architects and surveyors, 1; doctors and midwives, 3; barbers and hairdressers, 3; masseurs and oilers, 7; readers and entertainers, 3; bath attendants, 1; child nurses and attendants, 5; bodyguards, 10; table servants, 1; cooks, 3; provisioners, 2; caretakers, 10; gardeners, 4; social organizers, 1; animal tenders, 2; runners and bearers, 16; financial agents, 7; administrators, 11; secretaries and copyists, 7.

The full total over sixty years would have been in the thousands – and those are just the slaves.

THE HISTORIAN LIVY

Livy (Titus Livius) was born in Padua and moved to Rome in the 30s BC. A man of independent means, he took no part in politics and committed his life to writing. He lived at the time when the mighty Roman republic was in the process of being destroyed by the fight for power between ruthless dynasts like Julius Caesar, Pompey and Crassus, with private armies, underpinned by massive wealth, at their backs. The result of that dreadful civil war was the emergence in 27 BC of Caesar's heir Octavian as the first Roman emperor, under the name Augustus.

Livy's master work was his 142-book history of Rome (only thirty survive in full), which tells Rome's story from its foundations up to the time of writing in the first century BC. He greatly admired the achievements of the early Romans and was not in favour of emperors – too reminiscent of the hated Roman kings who had preceded the republic.

SPQR

Romans described themselves publicly as *SENATUS POPULUSQUE ROMANUS*, 'the Senate and the [whole] Roman People'. The term *populus* referred to 'the people, the state, the general public'.

Note: I shall use *pleb* for a single *pleb*, and *plebs* as the plural. In Latin, *plebs* is a *single* pleb, and *plebes* is the plural.

A RELIABLE HISTORY?

Livy acknowledged that the history of early Rome read more like poetry than proper history. But if Romans thought the war god Mars had been Rome's first parent, he said, fine! It certainly added dignity to Rome's story, and you might as well go along with it. After all, every nation at the time he was writing went along with Rome's *dominion* over them.

For the Romans, history began in 753 BC when the city of Rome was founded by Romulus. Livy agreed that there was little firm evidence for the accounts of the very early period, but his main interest was the story of Rome's moral decline, because 'the study of history is the best medicine for a sick mind'. It alone could provide examples of both what to do and what not to do to return Rome to its glory days.

Livy ends his introduction by expressing the hope that his passion for Rome has not impaired his judgement. No country, he claims, has ever been greater and richer in citizens and good deeds, none so free from greed and luxury, nowhere so content with plain living and even poverty, which in those long-lost days went hand in hand with contentment.

But greed, self-indulgence and every form of sensual pleasure have, it seems to him, led to an almost universal political death wish. He agrees that such caustic observations might not win much applause, but hopes that his efforts will be successful. That they have been is suggested by the fact that we still draw extensively on him some 2,000 years later.

Inevitably, Livy's history is full of very serious historical problems. But in this book, it is *his*-story that counts (groan: 'history' actually derives from the Greek *historia*, 'enquiry, research'). Consequently, I shall skate round all the problems that his superb account throws up. The speeches he cites, inevitably, are all invented, but they are brilliant examples of the way Romans understood what was at stake.

ENDNOTE

I have translated the Roman political ranks in general as 'officials', rather than 'magistrates' (Latin *magistratus*), to avoid confusion with our use of that term.

Roman politics was a complex and highly competitive business, involving many annually appointed officials (most offices lasting for one year only), interacting with an established Senate of 600 men drawn from the wealthy elites, and assemblies involving the whole body of male Roman citizens. These features will be described as the story develops.

sesterce (*ss* = *sesterces*): a Roman coin. A Roman soldier was paid 900*ss* a year in the first century AD.

as (pl. *asses*): there were four *asses* to a *sesterce*

denarius: equal to four *sesterces*

The famous 'Seven Hills' of Rome are in fact long ridges, already occupied hundreds of years before Romulus appeared. I shall call them 'ridges' from now on.

I

THE FIRST FOUR KINGS OF ROME:

753–616 BC

THE SACK OF TROY

The traditional date for the foundation of Rome is 753 BC, but the Romans' *story* about themselves actually started in a murky past long before that, with a Greek epic about the Trojan War. This – if there really was a Trojan War – probably happened around 1200 BC, when the Greeks laid siege to Troy to win back Helen, the most beautiful woman in the world, who had been seduced back there by the Trojan prince, Paris.

The story of Rome – the Romans believed – began with the successful Greek sack of Troy. That was the moment when the Trojan hero Aeneas managed to escape the slaughter and, after many adventures across the Mediterranean, finally landed in Italy.

There, it was claimed, he was destined to found not Rome but the Latin race – 'Latin' because the area in which they landed was called Latium, its inhabitants were called *Latini*, and they all spoke – you've guessed it – Latin.

ROMULUS: THE MYTHICAL BACKGROUND

So who actually *founded* Rome? The answer is, of course, Romulus. But how does he fit into the Aeneas story?

When Aeneas arrived in Italy, he had to fight his way to power. He founded the city of Alba Longa, and his male descendants became its kings. The last king of Alba Longa was Numitor, who had a daughter, Rhea Silvia. But Amulius, Numitor's brother, deposed him and promptly made Rhea a Vestal Virgin to prevent her continuing Numitor's line.

Rhea was raped by the god Mars, however, and produced twins. Wicked Amulius gave orders for them to be put in a basket and floated off down the Tiber to the sea (rather like Moses). But the basket came ashore near what would be the site of Rome. There the twins crawled out and were suckled by a she-wolf.

They were eventually found by a herdsman, a good, honest *pleb*, who named them Romulus and Remus. They grew up under his loving care, discovered who their real father was, overthrew wicked Amulius and restored Numitor to the throne.

THE FOUNDING OF ROME

The twins then decided to leave Alba Longa to found a new city on the very spot where they had come ashore. Being twins, neither had priority, so they invoked the gods to reveal who should rule. When Romulus claimed victory, a quarrel broke out between the brothers and he killed Remus. But Livy adds that there is another version of the story: Romulus killed Remus because he mocked the pathetic size of the walls that Romulus was building.

So the new city was called *Roma* – Rome – after Romulus.

STRONGMAN ROME

Romans greatly admired almost everything about the
ancient Greeks (except their democracy, which they saw as
mob rule) and loved to make as many connections as they
could with them. It is not surprising that some Romans
pointed out that *Roma* sounded rather like *rhômê*, the Greek
word for 'strength'.

The Romulus tale looks to be a pretty grim foundation story.
But the Roman world was very different from ours. Having the
god of war as your founder's father, who was suckled by a wolf,
surely gave you licence to ruthlessly conquer in a world in which the
ownership and control of territory were the keys to power.

At the same time, the hero Aeneas was a connection with the
ancient Greek world. This was valuable in the eastern Mediterranean
at the time: the famous Greeks had been settling in parts of Italy
from the eighth century BC.

Aeneas was also known for his *pietas*, a word that is the source of
our 'piety' and 'pity'. For Romans it meant respect for the family,
country and gods – exactly what was needed to justify Rome's
military conquests. Then again, observe the crucial part that was
played in Rome's history by a common herdsman – a *pleb* if ever
there was one – in saving the twins and raising them to become
fine men.

THE DUTIES AND RESPONSIBILITIES OF ANCIENT ROMAN PRIESTS

As guardians and overseers of religious law, customs and the sacred calendar, priests supervised temples and their staff and property and other sacred spaces and objects. Virtually all of them already existed in the period of the kings, though we cannot be sure of what their precise roles were. Virtually all were male and appointed for life.

But they did not act as beacons of moral virtue, like modern priests, nor as mediators between men and gods. If anyone did that, it was the Senate, which was responsible for banning (or accepting) foreign cults, responding to reports of prodigies and miraculous events, and so on. No surprise, then, that priests were senators and held major public offices. They were deeply entwined with the political world. Julius Caesar (d. 44 BC) is a fine example – he was elected to the post of *Pontifex Maximus* (see below).

FUNCTIONS

1. Priests conducted religious rituals and public animal sacrifices, libations, etc., to honour the gods, especially at festivals for the gods and times of crisis.

2. They interpreted the will of the gods through auspices (p. 40), omens, and the entrails of animals, as a result of which they advised officials as to the best course of action.

3. They organized regular annual celebrations in honour of the gods, many centred around the agricultural year, and ensured they were properly carried out.

4. They were subject to political manipulation if their activities were felt to threaten the careers of ambitious Romans, especially during the breakdown of the late republic.

SOME PERSONNEL

1. *Pontifices* (pontiffs), headed by the *Pontifex Maximus* (chief priest), advised the Senate on all aspects of state religion, the calendar and the law, and kept records of religious events and prodigies. Numbered up to sixteen. Originally co-opted, some were elected.

2. *Augures* (augurs) offered interpretations of the divine will through bird signs and natural phenomena in relation to public decisions, wars and elections. Numbered up to sixteen. Originally co-opted, some were elected.

3. *Flamines* (flamens) ran the cults of Jupiter, Mars and minor deities, under strict rules of dress and behaviour. One for each god. Chosen by the *Pontifex Maximus*.

4. Vestal Virgins: see p. 121.

5. *Fetiales* (fetials) handled religious protocol in foreign diplomacy, and declared war and concluded treaties with sacred rituals. There were twenty.

6. *Quindecimviri sacris faciundis*: these 'fifteen men for performing sacred rites' were in charge of the Sibylline Books (p. 90) and foreign cults.

ROMULUS 753–716 BC: THE START OF THE STORY

The dates of the early kings are the traditional ones. Given that each of them seems to have ruled for more than thirty years – extremely unlikely! – they bear little connection to reality. Whatever the truth about the very early years of Rome, there is no doubt that by 550 BC Rome was an established, powerful city.

Further, it is simply not the case that Rome was founded in the eighth century BC. Archaeologists have demonstrated beyond any doubt that this part of Italy had already been inhabited for hundreds of years before its traditional foundation date. The whole story of Romulus, then, is an invention, but it gives a fascinating insight into the mentality of those Romans who invented it – whenever that was!

SURVIVAL

The Romans lived in a fiercely competitive world, in which man was constantly fighting for survival against man, and winning meant everything.

Here, then, was Rome, a new boy on the block, attempting to make a space for itself in territory already fought over by many well-established communities. They would be Rome's prime enemies – the local clans or tribes of Latium (Latins) like the Albans and

Gabii, and those who surrounded them, such as the wealthy and powerful Etruscans (and their magnificent towns such as Veii), and others like the Aequi, Sabines, Volsci and Hernici (map, p. xi). They were watching Rome's development extremely carefully, and saw the advantage in weakening Rome, destroying it or even taking it over, as soon as possible.

EXPANDING THE CITY

Romulus' first job was to summon his subjects and give them some basic laws, 'without which there could be no unified body politic'.*

Realizing that he was ruling over a pretty rough collection of *plebs* and that some sense of dignity about his person could be useful, he created twelve special attendants (lictors) to go with him wherever he went.

LICTORS

Each of the lictors carried with him the *fasces* (source of our 'fascist'): a bundle of rods enclosing two axes that was a symbol of royal power, indicating what would happen to anyone who refused to obey orders – whipping or beheading. When the republic began in 509 BC, it was ordained that the two consuls should each be in charge (via his lictors) of the *fasces in turn*, so that only one consul at a time possessed that absolute power over life and death.

---

* When unreferenced words and phrases appear in quote marks, they are quotations taken directly from Livy.

Since Rome needed people to survive, Romulus threw his new city open to all comers as a place of security, an asylum for anyone from any clan who wished to migrate there: free, slave, fugitive, vagabond, criminal, layabout – any Tom, Dick or Harry (inevitably male: Romulus needed fighters) who fancied making a new life for himself. This was an extremely daring move. Ancient Greek cities, for example, would never dream of 'corrupting' themselves by welcoming in such people. But Rome was very different.

The invitation to newcomers succeeded, and Romulus now had to work out how to rule the city. He divided the Romans into three tribes for voting purposes, but as Rome expanded these became thirty-five. Each tribe made its decision on any topic by the majority vote. Romulus then decided that he needed an advisory body with the power to make laws. So he selected 100 individuals from the top clan families that made up the Roman people, to become *patriciani* ('patricians' or 'fathers'). This is where Rome's *internal* squabbles – *who rules?* – began.

WHERE DOES GROWTH COME FROM?

But there was another urgent problem to solve. The population of Rome was predominantly male. How was it to grow? Being a traditionalist, Romulus decided that the old methods were best, and invited any women from the surrounding clans, of which there were very many, to come and join them in this exciting adventure.

That did not go down well with those clans – who were rightly fearful of the speedy growth of this new foundation – or with their womenfolk, who did not like the look of the collection of scruffs that Romulus seemed to have gathered around him.

So Romulus invited the clans to a magnificent festival in honour of Neptune, the god of (among much else) horses (a horse was the equivalent of a Ferrari in the ancient world). The locals – including the powerful Sabine clan – came flooding in, women and all, to enjoy the spectacle. But as the festival started, the young Roman *plebs* raced out from the crowd and each seized the woman of his choice.

FESTIVALS

For most Romans, holidays at home were the rule. These were taken during public festivals, many of which were dedicated to the worship of the gods, especially the gods of nature, for the obvious reason that if nature failed, you were dead. Festivals – all times of relaxation – multiplied, expanded and began to run together. The line was finally drawn at 135 such days a year (at one stage it was 177!).

The festival broke up in panic. Romulus went round the women, assuring them that the men's intentions were wholly honourable, and that marriage was their objective. The young men too played their part, protesting that they had been overcome with irresistible love. ('No plea can better touch a woman's heart,' Livy sagely observes.)

This infamous story of the 'rape of the Sabine women' is certainly fictitious. As was made clear earlier, we know what Livy did not: that Rome had been occupied for hundreds of years before 'Romulus' ever arrived on the scene.

TALASSIUS

A very attractive girl was being dragged off by a group of rather rough men who, when challenged about what they were doing, said they were taking her to their excellent young friend Talassius to be his wife. This action was greeted with approval, and the name 'Talassius' was taken up and shouted by the attending crowd. That, we are told, is why *'Talassio'* ('for Talassius') was shouted at Roman marriages, while the bride 'against her will' was being carried across the threshold.

When the clans who had lost their womenfolk launched a revenge attack, the Romans were ready for them and beat them back. Another clan, uninvolved in the festival, decided to take advantage of this to seize any Roman land temporarily undefended, but they were quickly dealt with too. This pattern of action would be seen frequently down the centuries. It was at once clear that the Romans were not going to be pushovers.

The powerful Sabines, however, were a different prospect from the other clans. They planned an attack on the new city itself, and reached as far as the Citadel, a spur of the Capitoline ridge.

THE TARPEIAN ROCK

Tarpeia was the daughter of the commander of the Citadel and was bribed into showing the Sabines access to it up a steep path of the Capitoline ridge. It was said that she had asked to be given as a reward what they wore on their shield (left) arms, i.e. gold bracelets and jewelled rings. But after she had shown them the way, the Sabines crushed her to death with their shields, 'giving' her their shield arms in a way she had not expected. That part of the Capitoline came to be known as the Tarpeian Rock, off which traitors and criminals were thrown.

After ferocious fighting, the Romans managed to drive the Sabines out. At that point, the Sabine women who had been taken as wives appealed to their men, saying that they were now mothers and that their sons were Sabines too. Peace was made, and the Romans and Sabines united under a single government, with Rome as the seat of power. Small beginnings…

THE ETRUSCANS

The Etruscans, Rome's neighbours to the north, dominated northern Italy. Rich in mineral resources, by the eighth century BC they were attracting traders from the Greek world, from whom they developed their alphabet. (And the Romans developed their alphabet, which became ours, from the Etruscans.) Their magnificently decorated tombs were filled with luxury artefacts, indicating impressive levels of wealth through trade. Their interest in expanding their power was demonstrated by the backing they gave to the Etruscan Tarquinii, who were to rule Rome as kings for many years (see p. 38 ff.).

The next people to take on Rome were from Fidenae, an Etruscan town only six miles away. Their aim was to do as much damage as they possibly could, devastating the surrounding countryside and the farms. The Roman farmer-*plebs* fled into the protection of the city, where the alarm was raised and Romulus gathered fighting men and marched out. He set an ambush and lured the enemy troops towards it. Caught in this pincer movement, Rome's attackers fled back to Fidenae.

That prompted another far more powerful Etruscan city – Veii (ten miles from Rome) – to try its luck, and its men entered Roman territory, seizing what they could to take back home. The Romans got wind of this, drove them back, devastated their territory, and took control of some of their land. Veii promptly sued for peace and was granted a truce for a hundred years. Rome would not be at war for another forty years.

THE EARLY ROMAN ARMY

By now it seems as if a military unit had been formed, presumably consisting of the king, his bodyguard, retainers, and selected *plebs* from Rome's various clan groups. They were probably armed with iron-tipped spears and protected with leather corselets – and possibly metal chest plates – and shields. They would have fought as a phalanx, drawing themselves up in a line and charging at the enemy (legions were a long way off, c. 350 BC). The wealthy *equites* (compare 'equestrians', Latin *equus*, 'horse') made up the cavalry units, bringing a different dimension to the army's capabilities. They all presumably underwent training of some sort, so that by c. 550 BC they were a formidable outfit. But a fully paid, standing army would take another 700 years!

THE DISAPPEARANCE OF ROMULUS

These successes made Romulus more loved by the *plebs* and his personal armed guard of 300 men than by the patricians, Livy tells us – presumably the patricians thought they should be running the show. But then, suddenly, Romulus was heard of no more. While he was reviewing his troops, a storm burst, a cloud enveloped him, and he disappeared from sight. (We are still obviously in mythical territory here.)

There was now a suspicion among the *plebs* that the patricians had somehow done away with him. According to Livy, one Proculus Julius asked to address an assembly of *plebs* and claimed that Romulus had appeared to him with a message for the Romans from the gods: that Rome would be the capital of the world; that they should learn to be soldiers, and teach their children that no force in the world would be able to resist Roman arms. This calmed the situation.

ROMULUS: AN ASSESSMENT

Whatever we want to make of Livy's obviously fictional story of Romulus, Rome had the potential to grow fast. Its seven ridges made for a highly defensible settlement. They provided tufa (a soft limestone ideal for small-scale building) in great quantities; good deposits of clay (for tiles, pottery, etc.) were available round the bases of some of the ridges; the land itself was marshy and malaria-ridden, which probably added an element of protection; and the Tiber river was fordable where the city was built. There is a reason why it had been inhabited for so long before the Romulus myth: it had serious potential.

APPOINTING A KING: THE ROLE OF THE PLEBS

The patricians were soon quarrelling about who would be their next leader. The Sabines (many now living in Rome after the seizure of their women) wanted someone of Sabine blood, the Romans of Roman. But it was important to appoint someone quickly, because they knew they were surrounded by enemies.

The patricians decided that they themselves should exercise joint control, ten at a time. This did not satisfy the *plebs*, however, who said that this proposal brought them 100 masters (the patricians) rather than just the one they'd had before. They wanted a king back.

The patricians then reached a compromise: the *plebs* could elect a new king as long as their choice satisfied the patricians – the first inkling of plebeian power. This was acceptable to the *plebs*, who in fact decided to let the patricians make the choice.

KING NUMA: 715–672 BC

The patricians concluded that Rome's second king should be Numa Pompilius, a man famed for his justice and piety – and a

Sabine, not a Roman. Livy seems to have thoroughly approved; he writes that the Sabines were known as the most incorruptible of men.

A FARMER'S LIFE

Note: Since farming was so central to ancient life – where else could they get food from? – these boxes will discuss various aspects of it.

The farm should be in a safe neighbourhood because of the dangers of brigands, close to markets for selling one's products and buying what one could not produce oneself, with good access to them by road and water, and surrounded by farms in good condition.

Varro (encyclopaedist, c. 40 BC)

AN INTERNATIONAL WORLD?

The choice of Numa was a moment of great importance, and not just as the first signs of *pleb* power. We have already seen how Romans were perfectly happy to let peoples of all types and conditions become Roman. The crowning of a Sabine confirmed that this applied to their leaders as well. Unlike Greeks, Romans seem relaxed about welcoming in those from other cultures, even as a king – as long as he ruled in *their* interests and not anyone else's. That the gods approved of Numa Pompilius was made clear when the auguries all agreed.

AUGURIES

An augur was a religious official with expertise in interpreting divine pleasure or displeasure by the movement of birds. Another name for him was *auspex* (compare our 'auspicious'). The augur would stand on a high hill, facing south, hold a knotless stick in his right hand, offer a prayer to the gods, and mark out a space of the sky (using landmarks) into the four quarters of the compass. He would then transfer the stick into his left hand and watch that space: birds flying left to right were propitious, right to left unpropitious. The noises the birds made and the number of birds were also significant.

CONFIRMING THE PEACE

Rome was now at peace, and Numa determined that there was only one way to keep it like that, which was to breed into the uncouth Roman *plebs* a fear of the gods. Assorted priesthoods and ceremonies were introduced, and Livy tells us that, as a result, Rome's neighbours considered it to be almost an act of sacrilege to attack them!

One decision Numa took was to build a temple to Janus, the two-faced god of beginnings and endings, transitions and gates (Latin *ianua*, 'door'; compare 'January', the month that looks backwards and forwards). This temple was to be a visible sign of the alternation between war and peace: when its doors were open, it was war; when they were closed, it was peace.

Numa proceeded to conclude alliances with all the neighbouring communities, and the temple doors were closed for the entirety of his reign.

REORGANIZING THE YEAR

Originally the Romans had only ten months in their year, beginning in March (that explains our *September*, *October*, *November*, *December*, from the Latin for seven, eight, nine, and ten). This was probably because no fighting took place in January and February, the weather being bad and crops impossible to grow (armies on campaign had to live off the soil). Numa altered the calendar to begin in January, possibly because he placed such importance on the god Janus.

CONTROLLING THE MOB

The Greek historian Plutarch (d. c. AD 120) described Rome as being in a 'turbulent' state when Numa was appointed, because its reckless and daring people, coming from all sorts of backgrounds and locations, rejoiced in dangerous battles and campaigns. But Numa, a man of peace, regarded war and injustice as inseparable, and set about taming their fearsome and warlike tempers.

First, he instilled in them superstitious fears about the mysterious ways of the gods, and then – by introducing them to sacrifices, processions, religious dances and other agreeable diversions – he gradually won them over.

He also decreed that, while sacred ceremonies were being performed, the citizens should rid the streets of noise, clatter and clamour and everything connected with manual labour. Plutarch claimed that this continued up to his day: when the auspices or a sacrifice were taking place, the people cried out, 'Pay attention to this!'

Further, Numa took particular care to divide up free land among the poorest *plebs*. This saved them from destitution and therefore from wrongdoing, and at the same time instilled in them a desire for peace.

WORK

The Roman aristocrat Pliny the Younger (d. c. AD 113), recommending a young man to a friend of his, said: 'He loves hard work as much as poor people usually do.' Hardly surprising – for the poor, work meant surviving for another week or so.

In order to deal with what could be disruptive clan divisions, later writers tell us, Numa also organized the *plebs* into groups defined by their arts and trades – musicians, goldsmiths, carpenters, dyers, leatherworkers, braziers and potters – and the rest into a single, unified body of workers, all with their own social gatherings, public assemblies and so on. Numa's purpose, we are told, was to heal clan divisions.

But the peace did not last. When Numa died and the people voted for Tullus Hostilius – a Latin (i.e. from the region of Latium), not a Roman – to become their third king, there was a dramatic shift in policy.

672–640 BC: KING TULLUS HOSTILIUS

A number of cattle-raids had been going on between Alba and Rome, which Tullus decided to turn into a cause for full-on war.

However, the Alban leader Mettius pointed out to Tullus that the powerful Etruscans would be watching closely, hoping that both sides would badly weaken themselves, leaving both Romans and Albans easy prey. Should they rethink the matter?

THREE AGAINST THREE

As luck would have it, the armies of both sides contained youthful, energetic patrician triplets, the Roman Horatii and the Alban Curiatii. It was decided to reach a decision by letting *them* fight it out.

When the Curiatii's ruthless finishing (off) established a handy 2–1 lead, the last Horatius took to his heels and the two Curiatii, foolishly strung out behind, gave chase. As they caught up with Horatius, he picked them off one after the other.

But on returning home in triumph, Horatius found his sister in tears and loudly lamenting. She was calling out the name of one of the now-dead Curiatii – the man she had been in love with. Infuriated, Horatius killed her.

A FARMER'S LIFE

The herdsmen must be forced to stay in the pasture all day, to let the herds pasture together, but to spend the night alone, each with his own herd. Neither old men nor young boys can easily tolerate the difficult terrain and the steep and rugged mountains, although herdsmen must endure these hardships, especially herdsmen who follow cattle and goats which love to pasture on sheer cliffs or in thick forests.

Varro

THE PEOPLE DECIDE

In the circumstances, it is not surprising that Tullus himself shrank from demanding the death sentence for Horatius. He summoned the whole Roman people to an assembly, and in front of them commanded the appropriate legal authorities to make their decision. The death penalty it was.

But it was made clear that the prisoner was allowed to appeal to the people, and Tullus urged Horatius to do so. Horatius responded, and so did his father, who argued that his daughter had deserved death, but how could the death of his own son be right, when he had saved the Roman people from catastrophic defeat?

Moved by this appeal, the people decided that Horatius should be acquitted, but to mitigate the stain of the murder religious rituals should be carried out. And so it was done. Yet again, the *plebs* were actively involved in a political – and, this time, legal – decision.

METTIUS TURNS TRAITOR

The Albans were furious with their leader Mettius at the loss of their three brothers to the Romans. In response, Mettius persuaded the Etruscan people of Fidenae and Veii that, despite treaties with Rome, he would join them in an attack on their old enemy. When the attack was launched, Tullus naturally demanded that Mettius, in accordance with their treaty, join up with the Romans. Betraying both sides, Mettius deployed his troops but withdrew them into the ridges.

In the event, the Romans were victorious, and when the action was over Mettius marched out to congratulate them. Tullus politely suggested that both armies assemble the next day for a sacrifice of thanks, at which the Romans paraded, fully armed, surrounding the Albans.

Tullus then publicly revealed the extent of Mettius' treachery and informed the defenceless Albans that he intended to destroy Alba and transfer the whole population to Rome, where they would enjoy full citizenship and their elites would have the right to become patricians.

METTIUS MEETS HIS FATE

Tullus then turned on Mettius. Two chariots were drawn up back-to-back, each pulled by four horses. Mettius was strapped between them with ropes. At a touch of the whip, the two teams raced off in opposite directions. Mettius was ripped in half, the pieces of his body carried off in the ropes.

Alba was torn down and its displaced citizenry doubled the population of Rome. The Alban infantry and cavalry squadrons were added to the Roman army. The Roman council chamber was also expanded to allow for the new influx of Alban patricians.

The Sabines reckoned an attack on Rome at this fraught time might be profitable. They invited Veii to join them, and a few men volunteered to serve, 'together with some paupers and vagabonds persuaded by the chance of some pay'. Such desperation must have been common among *plebs* everywhere. However, the Sabine attack failed.

640–616 BC: KING ANCUS MARCIUS

After that a plague struck Rome. It killed Tullus, and the *plebs* appointed not a Roman but the Sabine Ancus Marcius, grandson of Numa, as their fourth king. The first thing that Ancus did was to create an official ceremonial for declaring war. The final decision was to be taken by the whole people: the 'elders' – the patricians – voting first, then 'in order', the *plebs*.

ANCUS CONQUERS AND ABSORBS THE LATINS

Inevitably, some surrounding Latin clans decided it was time to test Ancus and Rome's mettle. But Ancus took the Latin cities by assault and again transferred their citizenship to Rome.

Of the seven ridges, the Palatine was settled by the Romans, the Capitoline and Citadel by the Sabines and the region around the Caelian by the Albans. The Aventine was now occupied by the Latins, and the Janiculum area across the Tiber, linked to Rome by a wooden bridge, was fortified for the first time as a defence against an attack from the west.

The influx of new citizens into Rome caused a rise in criminal activity and a prison was built near the Forum. At the same time, Rome started expanding its own domains, seizing the land between the city and the sea and establishing Ostia on the Tiber as its main harbour, eighteen miles away, as well as some salt works.

SALT WORKS

Salt was highly coveted as a preservative and flavouring, and very expensive. The Romans used lead salt pans to produce it by evaporation from brine. Thanks to inscriptions on the pans, we know the names of some salt makers, for example Viventius, Veluvius and Cunitus. But Roman soldiers were not paid in salt: that old canard is down to Pliny the Elder (d. AD 79), who thought that the Latin word *salarium* (pay for a civil or military official) derived from *sal* ('salt').

II

THE LAST OF
THE KINGS:

616–509 BC

616–578 BC: KING TARQUINIUS PRISCUS

Ancus ruled for twenty-four years and retired. He was replaced by
Rome's fifth king, Tarquinius Priscus, who was not a Roman but
an ambitious, wealthy and hospitable young man with an equally
ambitious wife, from the town of Tarquinii (modern Tarquinia) in
the extremely powerful region of Etruria to the north.

This was significant. The Etruscans might have been tempted to
destroy Rome. Possibly they felt it more profitable to take it over.
To have one of their own in charge was at least a start.

ETRUSCAN INFLUENCE

We have already seen Rome's openness to political influences from
other peoples. Tarquinius is an interesting example. His father was
apparently a Greek master craftsman called Demaratus who had
been expelled from Corinth and came with three of his colleagues
to settle in Tarquinii, where he married and had children. He

was among a number of Greeks who had a powerful influence on Etruscan – and thus Roman – artistic culture.

Tarquinius made his mark in Rome, especially with Ancus, and, on the strength of his record of public service, the *plebs* gave him an overwhelming vote of confidence. To strengthen his grip on power, he added 100 new men 'from lesser families' to the patricians, raising the membership to 200 and later 300. He was determined to have loyal allies in that important body. Some of these 'lesser families' were most likely the wealthy and well-connected of *plebeian* origin.

A FARMER'S LIFE: THE DONKEY (I)

Most agricultural experts have as their main consideration the small, common donkey in the purchase and maintenance of livestock. And this is not wrong, for even in a country that lacks pasture it can be content with a small amount of food and any kind of fodder, since it is either fed on leaves and thorns of brambles or is given a sheaf of straw, but it also *grazes* on straw, which is abundant in almost all regions.

Columella (d. AD 70)

DEVELOPING ROME, C. 600 BC

Tarquinius' first campaign was against the Latins, from whom he took so much booty that he was able to put on elaborate public games with special seating for the patricians and the wealthy cavalrymen (*equites*), featuring horse racing and boxing. These games were celebrated annually at the public's expense – a very popular move – and were the origin of the famous Circus Maximus. The Latin *circus* gives us our 'circuit' (it meant literally 'going round and round').

TAKING THE AUSPICES

Tarquinius opened up land around the Forum for private building sites, shops and porticos. On the military front, he doubled the size of the *equites* of the Roman army, having identified their lack as a particular weakness.

This caused a spat with the famous augur Attius Navius, who said that no change was possible unless the birds gave their consent (p. 30). Tarquinius challenged his expertise, inviting Navius to say what he (Tarquinius) was currently thinking of doing and whether it could be done. Navius took the augury and said it could be done. So Tarquinius told him to take a whetstone and cut it in half with a razor. Without a moment's delay, that is what Navius did. 'Whatever we may think of this story,' Livy goes on, Romans thenceforth always took the augury as an essential preliminary to any serious undertaking in peace or war.

Tarquinius successfully repelled an attack from the Sabines, taking control of much of their territory, and further expanded Roman control over many Latin cities while also bringing thousands of Latins into Rome. The *plebs*, by far the largest element in the army, played a major part in all these very successful operations.

With peace secured, Tarquinius now turned to developing the city of Rome and building drains, some of them doubling as sewers, to clear the floodwater from the malaria-ridden, low-lying areas around the Forum. At this time, the whole Forum was actually *raised* in height to help deal with the problem!

MALARIA

We know that this deadly fever, widespread across the ancient world, is caused by mosquitoes carrying a parasite (a discovery made as late as 1896 by the Italian doctor Giuseppe Mendini). The Roman poet Horace (d. 8 BC) talked of the onset of the malaria season, 'when every father and adoring mother grows pale with fear for their children'.

The ancient view was that 'bad air' (*mala aria* in medieval Italian) was the cause, a reasonable enough theory since the disease was associated with swamps. Much of Rome was low-lying and pretty marshy. The 250-mile-long Tiber flooded every four or five years, with a big one every twenty-five years or so – not helped if water also backed up from the sea. Floodplains like the Campus Martius were often swamped. So the main drain – the Cloaca Maxima, only incidentally a sewer as well – was constructed in this early period to make the Forum inhabitable.

Much later on, Cato the Elder (d. 149 BC) advised building farms in 'healthy' places, away from swampy land, and the architect Vitruvius suggested locating villas on high ground (as the Roman elite did on the ridges of Rome). But this option was not open to *plebs*. So they looked to the gods for help – especially Febris (literally 'Fever'), who long outlasted antiquity and even had a shrine in the Vatican.

The ancient historian Dionysius of Halicarnassus (d. c. 7 BC) gives a vivid account of the *plebs* labouring away at this building work, being paid with a moderate allowance of grain:

> Some were employed in quarrying stone, others in hewing timber, some in driving the wagons that transported these materials, and others in carrying the burdens themselves upon their shoulders, still others in digging the subterranean drains and constructing the arches over them and in erecting the porticos and serving the various artisans who were thus employed; and smiths, carpenters and masons were taken from their private undertakings and kept at work in the service of the public.

Skilled and unskilled *plebs* at work together.

CLOACINA

Cloacina meant 'purifier' and she was also the goddess of sewers. This may seem a bizarre sort of deity, but when one considers that the purpose of sewers is to keep the streets clean and so maintain the health of the population and make the city a pleasant place to live in, it is not surprising. Indeed, there was a shrine to Cloacina in the Roman Forum.

578–534 BC: KING SERVIUS TULLIUS

The death of Tarquinius led to something of a scramble for power, since the sons of the previous Sabine king Ancus had always resented the Etruscan Tarquinius seizing the throne.

But civil war was averted and Servius Tullius, born into Tarquinius' household in mysterious circumstances (he was not Etruscan, nor Roman), became Rome's sixth king.

FESTIVAL OF COMPITALIA

A *compitum* was a place where roads met, and the Compitalia was a festival organized by the local community on behalf of the gods of the local households (the *Lares*). The festival was said to have been instituted by Tarquinius to celebrate the birth of Servius – because one of the theories was that he was the son of a *Lar*!

So it was a street party. Everyone joined in, including the slaves, who were given a degree of liberty for the occasion. The elites came along too: the statesman Cicero (d. 43 BC) wrote to his friend Atticus about the importance of joining in this local festival: 'But we must talk about all this during our strolls at the Compitalia. Do remember the day before the festival: I will order the bath to be heated [p. 230 ff.], and Terentia [Cicero's wife] is going to invite Pomponia [Atticus' wife]. We will make your mother one of the party.'

It was held shortly after the Saturnalia festival, around what we know as Christmas.

ROME AS THE CAPITAL OF
THE LATIUM REGION

Rome now seemed to be in a very dominant military position in the region, and an agreement was made with the peoples of Latium to identify the city as the region's capital. A temple to Diana was built in Rome to confirm the pact. This was in direct imitation of the gigantic and extremely famous temple to Artemis built earlier by the Greeks in Ephesus – the first to be made completely of marble.

A FARMER'S LIFE: THE DONKEY (II)

It nobly puts up with bad treatment from an uncaring keeper, tolerates wounds and deprivation, and as a result keeps working better than any other animal. For it is used to work and hunger and is rarely affected by diseases. The many and necessary functions of this animal, which is so small, more than compensate for its proportions, since it can plough easy land with light ploughs, and pulls vehicles with no small weight.

Columella

A DEFINING MOMENT: THE CENSUS

To Servius is ascribed the initiative that laid the groundwork for the development of the republic.

He established the practice of a regular five-year census, when every Roman male, in public before the censor, had to state his full name, the name of his father or guardian, his place of residence, occupation, and financial worth – i.e. property and money (not income). Those who failed to attend were imprisoned or put to death. On the strength of that, every male would be placed into a grouping, or rank (*classis*), determined by his ability to pay for, and so bear, weapons, and also how much tax he would have to pay, if that had to be levied. It was the West's first rigidly controlled ranking system.

The top grade

This consisted of the richest citizens, in two groups:

- Patricians, the richest of all, formed the battle command group.

- The cavalrymen (*equites*/equestrians). These were divided into eighteen cavalry groups, with money from the Treasury to buy horses and a grant from rich widows to feed and maintain them.

The five *classis* grades

Below the top grade, the Roman *plebs* were divided into five numbered *classes*, defined by property and armour:

Classis	Minimum worth	Armour	Weapons
I	100,000*ss*	Helmet, round shield, greaves, breastplate	Spear, sword
II	75,000*ss*	Helmet, oblong shield, greaves	Spear, sword
III	50,000*ss*	Helmet, oblong shield	Spear, sword
IV	25,000*ss*	[Oblong shield]	Spear, javelin, [sword]
V	11,000*ss*		Sling, stones [javelin]

Related categories

- Attached to *classis* I, two *classes* of engineers (who built bridges, siege engines, catapults, roads and so on, and in peacetime were employed on civilian projects).

- Attached to *classis* V, two *classes* of musicians (they played trumpets and horns to sound the alarm; to signal an attack, formation changes during battle, and changes of the watch; and to provide accompaniment to marching soldiers).

- Attached to no *classis*: the *proletarii*, the lowest group of all, were Romans who were so poor that all they could provide were offspring (*proles*), and were exempt from military service.

- Everyone knew which rank they belonged to and would move up or down if their property value rose or fell after each five-yearly census.

CLASS AND CLASSICS

'Class' derives from the Latin word *classis* (from a root meaning 'call, summon'). As we have seen, it meant one of the grades of citizen, defined by wealth. When, however, it was used as an adjective, *classicus*, it meant 'belonging to the top grade': that is, politically, to the patricians and *equites*, as above, and – in another usage – to the 'best orators, poets and other writers'.

RANK-BASED VOTING

But this move also involved a radical *political* change. For it was on the shoulders of the rich that those military burdens were mainly placed (the most expensive gear *and* the highest tax rates). So what was in it for the rich?

As Livy explains: 'While one man, one vote, implying equality of power and of rights, had been handed down by Romulus and the other kings, this new system, while it apparently still gave votes to every man, granted the political power to the leading citizens.' How come?

To put it very simply, when it came to appointing a consul, for example, under the new system Romans were divided by wealth into groupings called 'centuries'. These are nothing to do with 'hundreds', however! So let us call them 'colleges'.

Each college – just like the colleges voting for the president in America – voted to decide on the *single* candidate they wanted as consul. But here was the catch:

- The unnumbered 'top grade' group, together with those *plebs* in rank I, formed two 'colleges', with 98 votes.

- *All* the remaining ninety-five 'colleges' across the rest of the Roman male citizen population had 95 votes.

If, therefore, the wealthiest in society agreed between themselves on the man they wanted for consul, they got their way. Of even greater importance, the consuls and other officers of state would be elected for *one year only*.

Whenever this legislation actually came into play (it was sometime after the kings were expelled), rotation of office was seen by Romans as perhaps its most important feature. To allow consuls to remain in power for more than one year would threaten a return to kings holding power for years.

OFFICERS OF STATE
(*MAGISTRATUS* IN LATIN)

The Senate (*Senatus*) originally consisted of 100 patricians (leading families) selected by Romulus as advisers. This number rose to 300 and then, during the republic, to around 600 – each of them effectively appointed for life. All elected officials (see the following list) were members, as well as those selected by the censors (wealth was a critical factor). It was a deliberative and advisory body *only* – it did not pass laws directly (the people's assemblies did that) and had no statutory power – but its decrees on matters

of, for example, finance and state and foreign policy were
extremely influential and rarely challenged.

- Consuls, 509 BC: Two were appointed every year as
  supreme heads of state, exercising *imperium*, i.e. the right
  to give orders that had to be obeyed. They were accompanied by lictors (p. 21). They consulted and presided over
  the Senate, the main policy and law-proposing body (the
  Comitia Curiata, p. 62, passed the laws); presented bills
  to be ratified by the decision-making assemblies; and
  recruited armies, which they led into battle.

- Praetors, 367 BC: Responsible for the court system and
  in charge of private law cases concerning the rights
  of people and property. They too held *imperium*, were
  accompanied by lictors and were military commanders.
  They had the right to consult the gods through the
  auspices (p. 40).

- Quaestors, sixth century BC?: Romans speculated that
  these perhaps began under the kings as administrative
  assistants, perhaps with some legal authority, and then
  assisted the consuls. They had duties connected with the
  state treasury, its statutes and documents, and financial
  affairs. In the main their job was to support the holders
  of *imperium*, and they therefore had a wide range of
  responsibilities.

- Aediles, 494 BC: Appointed by the *Concilium Plebis* and the *Comitia Tributa*, they were responsible for the fabric of the city, the upkeep and cleaning of the roads and paths, the distribution of water, and public behaviour. They had responsibility for controlling prices, especially of corn. They also put on games and other large-scale public entertainments (e.g. chariot racing and gladiatorial shows) at their own expense, which could advance their political ambitions.

- Tribunes of the *plebs*, 494 BC: Their function was to preside at the Plebeian Assembly and to present bills to it for ratification, to assist any citizen who had been seized by an official, and to veto any proposal by an official or the Senate of which the Plebeian Assembly disapproved. They could also prosecute an individual on a wide range of charges, which would be heard before an assembly of all the people.

- Dictator, early fifth century BC: Appointed, usually by a consul, during emergencies, with absolute authority to take charge of the state – and, to prove it, he was accompanied by twenty-four lictors. His period of office was limited to six months, and the other officials acted as his subordinates. The office disappeared after the Second Punic War (202 BC), but was briefly restored during the chaos of the first century BC (p. 188 ff.).

- Censor, 443 BC: p. 45.

The result of this division of responsibilities and limitation of tenure meant that it was very difficult for any one person to establish a real power base. Influence and authority, yes, but permanent, personal *imperium*, no. That would await the emperors.

THE RESULT OF THE CENSUS

The purpose of the census was to structure the whole of society – including the many 'new Romans' created by Rome's conquests – to create a group solidarity about its military responsibilities.

The long-term result of this reform was to turn Rome into the most formidable fighting force that the ancient world had yet seen. In politics and on the battle line, both patricians and *plebs* now knew exactly what their responsibilities were to each other and to Rome. In this respect at least, they were now all equal, with the same responsibility of confronting, within their newly defined duties, Rome's political and military battles.

At the same time, the armaments they possessed did away with any guesswork about what their individual role in battle would be. This sense of one's individual responsibility, enhanced by regular training and tactical awareness, provided the basis of a discipline unmatched among the other Italian tribes. It is, of course, perfectly true that the Roman army could be beaten. But if it was, there was no doubt about what would happen next: they would be back.

Likewise, the sheer amount of fighting that Rome had to do acted as serious training ground for the patricians of the Roman battle command group.

THE FOUNDING OF THE REPUBLIC?

But at this point, you might be saying: 'That is all very well, but Servius was the sixth king of Rome, and we know that Rome had seven kings. So what's all this about consuls already, then? What is going on?' The answer is – we don't know. Early Roman history is full of such problems. All we can say is that the 'Servian constitution' seemed to click in *after* the reign of the seventh and final king, in 509 BC. It was then that the patricians became senators, and the top power-brokers in Rome became the two annually elected consuls.

That, believed the Romans, was the start of their republic. It would last 482 years, from 509 BC to 27 BC, the year the first Roman emperor Augustus was proclaimed (during the chaotic period when Livy was writing his history).

SERVIUS OVERTHROWN

The young Lucius Tarquinius, son of the previous Etruscan king, Tarquinius Priscus, was keen to displace Servius and started rumours to suggest that Servius did not have the people behind him.

So Servius made another very significant move. He divided up *among the citizens* the land that he had gained by conquering enemy peoples. This went down very well with the *plebs* but was not so popular with the patricians, who regarded ownership of the land as their right – to be parcelled out in any way they chose.

Inevitably, Lucius Tarquinius took advantage of this move to whip up the 'lesser patricians' – those who had been appointed to the position by his father – and the wealthy, and then summoned a meeting of the patricians, taking the king's seat in front of their council chamber.

There he accused Servius of being in league with the lowest classes of society, robbing the wealthy with his latest land reforms and carving up precious land among the riff-raff of the poor. Servius disputed that claim, but Tarquinius picked him up and threw him down the steps of the patricians' chamber, where he was killed by Tarquinius' cronies.

534–509 BC: TARQUINIUS SUPERBUS, THE FINAL KING

In the chaos that followed, the Etruscan Lucius Tarquinius was declared Rome's seventh king, a man who came to be given the moniker *Superbus* ('haughty, arrogant, proud'). As king, Tarquinius S.:

- Refused burial to Servius.

- Executed those patricians who had not supported him.

- Appointed a bodyguard.

That last was a move always seen as the mark of the tyrant – a man who had come to power by force, unelected by the people, unsanctioned by any official authority, who could rule only by fear.

Tarquinius S. at once began to try people without any procedures, and condemn to death, exile or confiscation of property those he disliked:

- He drastically reduced the number of patricians and intentionally kept that body weak, ruling without consulting them.

- Alliances were broken or entered upon without the agreement of the patricians or the *plebs*.

STRENGTHENING ROMAN POWER

But Tarquinius S. was keen to bring the Latins on board, and made an agreement with them to combine the Latin and Roman armies. He rearranged the military units into equal numbers of Roman and Latin troops, with each unit under the command of a Roman centur--ion. The Latins were now fully on Rome's side, greatly expanding Rome's power and prestige. At least in this respect, Livy agrees, Tarquinius S. was a success. Further:

- He started waging war against the powerful Volsci, taking the fabulously wealthy town of Suessa Pometia (and then flattening it).

- He used its resources to fund the building of a magnificent temple to Jupiter on the Capitoline, one of the seven ridges of Rome (compare Capitol Hill in Washington, DC);

- He turned his attention to taking the neighbouring town of Gabii – which, Livy says, became so difficult that 'unlike a Roman, he had to rely on deceit and treachery'. But it worked, and Gabii became Roman.

ROMAN COLONISTS, C. 510 BC

Tarquinius S. now devoted himself to completing his gigantic temple of Jupiter. He called in workmen from Etruria and the poorer Roman *plebs*, who were happier working on the temple, Livy tells us, than they were slogging away at the Cloaca Maxima and building the Circus (pp. 41–2).

But there were still too many of the 'idle *plebs*' in Rome, who seemed to Tarquinius S. to be a burden on the city. So he sent them out as colonists to various locations around Rome, where they could guard the city by land and sea – in the process, of course, extending the frontiers of his dominions.

A FARMER'S LIFE: SLAVES

Do not appoint that idle and dreamy rank of slaves, accustomed to leisure, the countryside, the circus, theatres, gambling, taverns, and brothels. They never stop dreaming of the same trivialities, which when transferred to agriculture, lead to losses. Choose only someone who has been hardened by rural work from childhood and has been tested by experience, or someone who has endured laborious servitude.

Varro

THE KEY TO POWER:
KISSING YOUR MOTHER

There then occurred a terrifying omen: a snake slid out of the crack in a wooden pillar in his palace. Tarquinius S. decided that nothing less than a visit to the famous oracle at Delphi in Greece would be enough to assess its significance. So he sent off his two sons, accompanied by (Lucius Junius) Brutus, the son of his sister Tarquinia.

Brutus, knowing that he could not trust Tarquinius S., had from a young age pretended to be a dimwit, and had been happy to see all his possessions seized by the king and to be called Brutus (in Latin, 'thick as a brick'). Presumably Tarquinius S. thought his nephew's presence would be a way of keeping his sons amused on the journey.

When they had carried out their father's instructions, his sons could not resist asking the oracle which of them would succeed to the throne in Rome. The oracle replied, 'The man among you who first kisses his mother.'

The brothers kept this secret to themselves and agreed that, when they got back to Rome, they would draw lots as to who would kiss their mother first. But Brutus thought the oracle had a different meaning – and, pretending to stumble, he fell to the Earth and pressed his lips against it, regarding her as the common mother of all mortals.

509 BC: THE RAPE OF LUCRETIA
AND THE END OF THE KINGS

When the brothers returned, they found Tarquinius S. preparing for war against Ardea, a very wealthy town about twenty miles from Rome, near the sea. He needed the money to refill Rome's coffers after all his building, but also to appease the *plebs*, who had been kept hard at work like slaves on his various projects. The initial assault failed, and the Romans settled down to besiege the town.

One evening, a group of young elite soldiers were drinking and thought it would be fun to gallop back to Rome and see what their wives, caught unawares, were up to. So off they went – among them Sextus Tarquinius, one of Superbus' sons – to find most of their wives at luxurious banquets having fun with their friends. But not Lucretia, the wife of Tarquinius Collatinus. She was wool-working late at night, together with her slaves. Lucretia welcomed them in and fed them, and Sextus was captivated by her beauty and obvious chastity.

A few days later, without telling Collatinus, Sextus returned to the house and was as usual welcomed in, served dinner and shown to the guest chamber. That evening he raped Lucretia and fled. She sent messengers to Collatinus and her father that they should each come at once with a trusty friend: a terrible thing had happened.

Her father brought Publius Valerius; Collatinus brought Brutus. Lucretia described the event. They urged her to understand that it was the mind that sinned, not the body; where there was no intention, there was no guilt. But she said that she could not allow herself to live after such a disgrace and stabbed herself to death. Brutus seized the bloody dagger and swore to destroy Tarquinius S. and his family, come what may: 'I will never allow any of them, or anyone else, ever again to be King in Rome.'

And so it was done. All the Tarquins were driven out and two consuls were elected by the Servian method – Collatinus and Brutus. By this time, Rome had a population of about 40,000, occupying some 350 square miles – larger than any other city in the region.

CONCLUSION

Livy comments that kings had reigned Rome for 244 years from its foundation to its liberation, and that the theme of his history from now on would be 'Rome's achievements in peace and war, their annually elected officers of state and the construction of a legal system superior to the authority of men'.

Clearly, he saw annual rotation of office and a secure legal system as essential features of good government – and these were certainly not typical of the rule of the kings.

Nevertheless, for Livy it was to their credit that the kings had maintained control over what was in those early days of Rome something of a rabble. In fact, Livy judged Rome's rule by kings as a period of great importance because it fostered a political maturity whose 'ripened powers bore the *good* fruit of liberty'. Was that partly down to the fact that none of the early kings had been Roman (Romulus was from Alba)? All were brought in from outside. As has been noted already, that seems to have been one of Rome's greatest strengths.

Livy was less than enthusiastic about the Roman *plebs*. That seems slightly out of tune with some aspects of his account of early Rome. After all, on a number of occasions he mentions the *plebs'* involvement in making political and social decisions, and never seems to find them wanting in their willingness to fight in support of the kings' desire to enlarge the Roman state.

But perhaps, in making this overall critical assessment of the Roman *plebs* as a rabble, it is possible that he was looking to make comparisons with events in the Rome of his day, when law and order had almost entirely broken down.

But Livy does end his reflections on a positive note, when he describes how Brutus not only restored to 300 the number of the patricians in the Senate (after the Tarquins had murdered so many) but also looked *outside* the rank of 'patrician', i.e. to the *equites*, to do so. This meant that wealthy *plebs* were now in positions of power equal to the patricians. He concludes: 'This was wonderfully effective at promoting national concord and uniting *plebs* and patricians in a sense of common purpose' (something sadly lacking in Livy's day).

But the question was: whose side would those patrician-*plebs* now be on? In the event, that move was not enough to bring about a lasting peace between those two groupings, as Livy would go on to demonstrate as the struggle intensified.

Note: From this point on, Livy was able to date events by the consular *fasti*. These were the records kept of the names and dates of the Roman consuls, two of whom were elected for every year, and of other important officials, which went back to the start of the republic. There is every reason to believe that these were pretty reliable records, as were the events associated with them. From now on, Livy's account has a firmer historical basis.

III

THE FOUNDING OF THE REPUBLIC:

509–473 BC

THE PLEBS: AN IMPORTANT NOTE

However positive Livy felt about the introduction of wealthy *plebs* into the patricians, a far greater division in the ancient world was that between the rich and the poor. That is the really important distinction, because the poor not only vastly outnumbered the rich; they also made up the great majority of the troops fighting the battles that kept Rome safe, thereby extending Rome's control of resources and so wealth. That is what gave the poor their possible influence over events.

THE CLANS/TRIBES

Note: This guide gives some idea of the system as Livy himself would have understood it in the first century BC. Elements of it appeared perhaps as early as the sixth century BC.

Every Roman citizen belonged to a clan/tribe, by assignment or heritage, of which the number increased from three in Romulus' day to thirty-five (four urban tribes, thirty-one rural tribes). Freed slaves, who became partial citizens, automatically joined an urban tribe.

For the purpose of voting, citizens gathered in the Forum, or on the Capitoline ridge – or later, as Rome grew, on the Campus Martius (an area covering 600 acres, or roughly 340 soccer pitches). There they were grouped by tribe. They would know what the 'either/or' issue was because it had already been discussed in an assembly (see below).

Officials then asked each tribe in turn to vote for its decision, probably by raising hands, or shouting, or (from the late second century BC) by secret ballot. Voting ended as soon as eighteen tribes had made the same decision.

The two tribal decision-making assemblies were:

- The Comitia Tributa: This assembly of *plebs* and patricians elected lower officials (military tribunes, quaestors, aediles), enacted legislation proposed by officials, and adjudicated on non-capital cases, fines, appeals, etc. Voting was by tribe (*trib*-uta), not by wealth. That meant it was dominated by plebeian votes to create plebeian officials.

- The Concilium Plebis: This body, founded in 494 BC, passed plebiscites, laws relating originally just to the *plebs*, but after 287 BC to everyone; elected inviolate plebeian tribunes to protect the *plebs'* interests in the Senate; adjudicated on cases involving plebeians; and generally legislated to advance plebeian interests. It is sometimes known as the (Plebeian) Tribal Assembly.

The Comitia Centuriata worked differently. It elected the highest state officials (e.g. consul, praetor), passed laws, determined war or peace, heard appeals on capital trials, ratified censuses and dealt with religious issues. Its electorate consisted of all Roman citizens categorized by wealth into (eventually) 193 'colleges' (called 'centuries', hence the title). Each 'college' had one vote. The wealthiest 'colleges' numbered 98 and therefore controlled 98 votes. The remaining 'colleges' therefore numbered 95 votes. (On all this, see p. 48.)

How many citizens actually turned up to vote in the first century BC cannot be estimated. Guesses range from 5,000 to 20,000, from a population (more guesses) of 400,000–500,000. At the time we are dealing with here, Rome's population was around 40,000.

THE LAST OF THE TARQUINS

The first thing that Brutus did as consul was to propose that his fellow consul Tarquinius Collatinus be removed from office because of his associations with the Tarquins. He brought the issue before the assembly of the *plebs*, assuring Collatinus that he would lose none of his possessions and would still remain a friend. Collatinus finally agreed and went into exile, being replaced by Publius Valerius, who had been present when Lucretia killed herself (p. 57).

But some of the younger elite in Rome, who had enjoyed favours under King Tarquinius S., hatched a plot to have him returned. It was put into action, but the plan was overheard by a slave, information was laid before the consuls and the traitors were arrested. All the property belonging to the Tarquins in Rome was left to the *plebs* to pillage, the traitors were executed, and the slave was given Roman citizenship.

507 BC: PLEB POWER

Tarquinius S. was not going to put up with this and, alongside Veii, launched an attack on Rome. It was indecisive, but Brutus was killed in the battle, and the surviving consul Publius Valerius – who had not yet appointed a replacement for Brutus – was seen to be building a house on the top of a ridge that looked as if it was meant to be impregnable. The news got out and aroused suspicion in the minds of the *plebs* that he was planning to restore the monarchy.

Valerius therefore called a meeting of the *plebs* and, before he spoke, told his lictors to lower the *fasces* (the symbol of authority allowing the punishment of anyone disobeying authority: see p. 21).

Doing that in the presence of the *plebs* was taken to be a good sign, suggesting that it was the *plebs* in whom power was vested, not the consul. Valerius' speech won them over, and the material for building his house was brought down to ground level, where it was reconstructed.

Then, presumably because he was aware of the power that the *plebs* wielded, Valerius passed two measures that ingratiated him with them further:

- Anyone should have a right to appeal to the *plebs* against any decision made by a consul or other official.

- Anyone convicted of planning the return of the monarchy should lose all civil rights.

CARTHAGE

We are told that in 509 BC – the first year of the republic – this powerful North African city made a treaty with Rome, and more followed in 348 BC, 279 BC, 241 BC and 226 BC. The treaties mainly related to trading rights, piracy and ownership of territory. There would be no point in doing this if Rome were not actively engaged in trading around the western Mediterranean. This was important – for example, in the case of famine. Bread was the staff of life: getting access to sources of grain was a very high priority.

506 BC: HOW HORATIUS KEPT THE (SUBLICIAN) BRIDGE

Meanwhile, Tarquinius S. had persuaded the Etruscans that it was time to deal with Rome and restore the monarchy, and the job was given to Lars Porsena, the king of the Etruscan town of Clusium. This was a daunting prospect for Rome, and the Senate felt that the people, fearful of being defeated and sold into slavery, might be tempted to bring back the kings.

They therefore implemented a number of economic measures: controlling prices, removing tolls and taxes from the *plebs* that the rich would pay, and moving the Roman farmers back into the city. These initiatives were so successful that the people remained solidly united despite the deprivations (Livy comments that no democracy could ever have agreed to that).

The first Etruscan assault was ended by Horatius Cocles, who famously 'kept the bridge' – the only route into Rome over the Tiber. He and two companions did so by protecting the narrow entrance on the Etruscan side until the bridge was knocked down by the Romans behind them. His companions leapt back before it fell, leaving Horatius stranded.

Here is Lord Macaulay in his famous poem on that moment, 'Horatius' (Sextus is the man who raped Lucretia):

> Alone stood brave Horatius,
> But constant still in mind;
> Thrice thirty thousand foes before,
> And the broad flood behind.
> 'Down with him!' cried false Sextus,
> With a smile on his pale face.
> 'Now yield thee,' cried Lars Porsena,
> 'Now yield thee to our grace!'
>
> Round turned he, as not deigning
> Those craven ranks to see;
> Nought spake he to Lars Porsena,

To Sextus nought spake he;
But he saw on Palatinus
The white porch of his home;
And he spake to the noble river
That rolls by the towers of Rome.

'Oh Tiber, father Tiber,
To whom the Romans pray,
A Roman's life, a Roman's arms,
Take thou in charge this day!'
So he spake and, speaking sheathed
The good sword by his side,
And, with his harness on his back,
Plunged headlong in the tide.

Horatius, of course, survived. The Etruscans laid siege to the city, various heroic deeds were done, and the result was a peace treaty.

504 BC: APPIUS CLAUDIUS

Trouble with the Sabines broke out again, which Rome dealt with successfully, resulting in a large number of Sabines being welcomed into Rome as citizens and given land.

Among them was one Appius Claudius, who was made a patrician and quickly rose to eminence. Remember that name. He would turn out to be someone who had little time for the *plebs*.

495 BC: AFTER TARQUINIUS SUPERBUS' DEATH

The death of Tarquinius S. came as a great relief to the Romans but had one unfortunate consequence: now that the threat of a return to monarchical rule was no longer hanging over them, the Senate felt that they no longer needed to keep the Roman *plebs* – who made up the bulk of the army – happy. The result was a degree of oppression that the *plebs* had not experienced for some time.

THE PLIGHT OF THE PLEBS

The main problem for the *plebs* at this time was one of debt. It was illustrated by the appearance in the Forum of a *pleb* – emaciated, threadbare, unkempt, covered in weals – who had been so long fighting the enemy for the liberty of his country that he had not been able to protect his own farm. As a result, the enemy had ruined his crops, burned his cottage and seized his cattle.

A FARMER'S LIFE: IN PRAISE OF ITALY

What emmer [grain] is to be compared with that in Campania, what wheat with that in Apulia, what wine with that in Falernia, what olive oil with that in Venafrum? Is Phrygia [Turkey], which Homer calls 'vine-clad', more quickly covered with vines than Italy? Or Argos, which Homer calls 'rich in grain', more covered in wheat? In what other land does the *iugerum* [2/3 of an acre] produce 125 gallons of wine as some districts in Italy do?

Varro

In order to pay taxes, he'd had to take on debt. Interest on the debt increased, he lost the land that his grandfather and father had passed down, and, reduced to slavery, he was held in an underground prison – effectively a death sentence.

Many other debtors had had that experience. Many of them still in chains, they crowded into the Forum. It was soon filled with a noisy throng, all showing what they had suffered in return for the campaigns they had fought.

The two consuls tried to calm them but failed, and the crowd demanded that the consuls convene the Senate. Most of the senators had quietly disappeared, but the consuls, realizing the seriousness of the situation, managed to raise enough for the Senate to assemble. Of the two consuls, Appius Claudius was in favour of arresting a few of the crowd in order to calm them down through fear, while Publius Servilius thought it wiser to try to use persuasion and calm their fury.

In the middle of the debate, horsemen galloped up with news that the Volsci were advancing on the city. The *plebs* were delighted: the gods were punishing the Senate's arrogance. They urged each other not to sign up – let the senators do the fighting for a change. The Senate, terrified by the current situation and the impending attack, urged Servilius to see what he could do.

Servilius told the crowd that the senators were keen to do what they could for the *plebs*, but they could not do so with the enemy at the gates. If the *plebs* signed up to fight, he assured them, no action would be taken against them in relation to the debt problem.

This appeal was successful, and next day the Volsci forces were put to flight, and the troops rewarded with booty.

THE CONSULS SNUBBED

A temple to Mercury was being built and it needed to be dedicated. Who should do it? The Senate turned the decision over to the people, saying that their choice would be responsible for distributing the grain and establishing a sort of guild of merchants (Mercury was the god of business).

To the horror of the patricians, the people chose neither of the two consuls, but a centurion, Marcus Laetorius. In his history, Livy remarks that this was a clear snub to the consuls because of their refusal to deal with the debt problem, and a sign that the people were growing in confidence.

APPIUS CLAUDIUS: VIOLENCE ON THE STREETS

The *plebs* felt they had done their duty in defence of Rome, and invited Servilius and the patricians to deal with the debt crisis. The consul Appius Claudius would have none of that: he wanted to leave the *plebs* to the mercy of their creditors!

The situation then turned ugly. Knowing that they would receive no help from the Senate or the consuls, the *plebs* took matters into their own hands. They took advantage of the right of appeal against arrest – which the previous consul Publius Valerius had given them (p. 64) – and physically intervened when debtors were taken off to court, while shouting down any orders from the consul. Violence returned to the streets, and it was now the creditors who had to run for their lives from angry mobs. The discontent continued until Servilius and Appius both left office, the former humiliated but Appius held in high regard by the more conservative senators.

494 BC: DICTATORSHIP AVOIDED

Such was the distrust that the whole situation had created between *plebs* and Senate that the *plebs* started meeting in private to discuss what to do next. That set a very dangerous precedent – Romans addressed serious matters in assemblies, not in secret groups – and the senators wanted to know what the two new consuls would do about it. It was suggested that they should order a very strict levy of troops to take the *plebs*' minds off the debt problem. That was greeted by the *plebs* with the contempt that it deserved.

A FARMER'S LIFE: WET WEATHER

If rainy weather has caused a problem, remind the overseer he must take advantage of it: clean and re-pitch the storage jars, clean the farmstead, move the grain, haul out manure, tell the workers to mend their smocks and hoods. On feast days clear out old ditches, repair roads, cut down briars, dig over gardens, weed meadows, root up thorns, pound emmer, and generally tidy the place up.

Varro

Eventually Appius Claudius, whose hatred of the *plebs* was absolute, suggested that the Senate appoint a dictator: the law was that such a figure's orders were final, and there could be no appeal against him (p. 50). He would have been made dictator himself, to the fury of the *plebs,* but the older members of the Senate and the two consuls argued that the situation demanded moderation and appointed Manlius Valerius, brother of the Publius Valerius who had given them that right of appeal.

This was a man the *plebs* felt they could trust, and they immediately signed up for the army, since their old foes the Aequi, Volsci and Sabines were on the march again. Roman discipline won the battle, and more territory was taken over to be colonized by Roman *plebs*.

THE PLEBEIAN REVOLT

But these successes, welcome as they were, did nothing to solve the political struggle between moneylenders and their debtors. As dictator, Manlius Valerius immediately raised the question before the patricians, who refused to debate it.

Valerius warned them that the time would come when they would regret their refusal to face this problem; in the light of the Senate's decision to frustrate the hopes of the *plebs,* he could no longer remain as dictator, preferring to fight for the people's interests as a citizen. The Senate decided to play for time by ordering the army to take up arms again on the (false) grounds that an attack from the Aequi was impending. This created such a fury that there was even talk of assassinating the consuls. The situation was now very dangerous.

Persuaded that such a criminal act would solve nothing, the army fell in with the suggestion of a man called Sicinius. He proposed that they go on strike, up sticks and decamp in a body to the Sacred Mount across the Anio river, three miles from the city. There, having brought what they needed in the way of food, they pitched their tents and fortified their camp.

STRIKES

What have 'strikes' got to do with workers 'walking out'? The term was invented in 1768, when sailors in the port of Sunderland 'struck', i.e. removed, their sails, and refused to go back to work until they got better terms. The earliest known strike was in Egypt in 1152 BC, when royal tomb workers downed tools because their beer and grain rations were late.

This caused panic in Rome, among both the plebeians and the Senate. How long before that army on the Sacred Mount took up arms against Rome herself? And what would happen if there was a sudden invasion?

THE BODY AND THE STOMACH

It was therefore decided to send Menenius Agrippa, a plebeian by birth, as an ambassador to the deserting army, to try to persuade them to give up their strike. Livy reports the speech that Menenius was said to have given, 'in the quaint and uncultured fashion of the times', as follows:

In the old days, men's limbs did not all agree among themselves as they do now, but each had its own voice and ideas. The body then started complaining about all the trouble and effort it had to put into feeding the stomach, which just sat there in the middle of the body, doing nothing but enjoying the delicacies it was given.

So the body formed a plot that the hands would not deliver food to the mouth, that the mouth would not accept what it was given, and the teeth would not chew anything it received. But while their anger was aimed at starving the belly into submission, the only result was that the limbs and the whole body became weaker and weaker.

It then became obvious that the stomach's efforts served a purpose. It did not in fact get more food than the rest of the body, but it distributed, among the whole body, the means by which we live and flourish – that is, by the veins which carry the digested food to all parts equally.

By comparing the revolt of the body to the anger of the *plebs* against the Senate in this way, Menenius won the *plebs* over, and discussions began about an agreement that produced the following compromise:

- The *plebs* should have their own (two) inviolable 'tribunes of the *plebs*', appointed by an assembly of *plebs*.

- The tribunes would be above the law and so have the power to protect the *plebs* as a whole against the consuls.

- They would be able to veto *all* legislation.

- No patrician would be permitted to take that office.

These were the first moves in the 'Conflict of the Orders' (*plebs* vs. patricians; see p. 195) which over the years gave the *plebs* equality as a political force with the elites.

ANNA PERENNA

This was the name of a famous *pleb* festival, featuring lots of drinking and mostly controlled mayhem. Here is one version of how it came about.

When the army camped out on the Sacred Mount found themselves running out of food, a kind old woman, Anna – poor but a hard worker – took pity on them and started baking cakes for them, delivering them fresh every morning. When she died, a statue to her was erected and it was agreed to set up a festival in her honour for such kindness at such an important moment in Rome's history.

492–1 BC: FAMINE AND CORIOLANUS

That problems still remained was almost immediately illustrated by a severe famine caused by the secession of the *plebs* from their farms. The consuls sprang into action and sent agents out over a wide area to arrange for the purchase of grain. The situation was relieved by large supplies arriving from Sicily. The question now facing the Senate was the price the *plebs* had to pay for it.

Coriolanus, a superb soldier named after the town of Corioli – which he had taken almost single-handed – was one of the senators who thought that they ought to blackmail the *plebs* into giving up their new powers in return for cheap grain. The subsequent fury of the *plebs* was calmed by one of their tribunes, who issued a summons against Coriolanus, effectively leaving his fate in the *plebs'* hands.

TRIBUNES AND THE SENATE

The tribunes of the *plebs* were not allowed to enter the Senate house; seats were placed for them outside the doors. The tribunes used to examine the decrees of the Senate very carefully and, if they disapproved of any of the decrees, they would not allow them to be passed into law. The letter C [Latin *censeo*, 'I recommend'] used to be written at the bottom of ancient Senate house decrees. This mark meant that the tribunes had recommended them.

Valerius Maximus (author of a volume of *Memorable Deeds and Sayings* from Roman and Greek history,

c. AD 30)

The Senate tried to resolve the situation but failed – and, in the event, Coriolanus did not appear in court. He was condemned to exile and, vowing vengeance on his own country, went off to join the Volsci. There he linked up with Attius Tullius, a lifelong enemy of Rome, and together they prepared their plans for war.

They set up a complicated deception, involving the Romans allowing the Volsci to be admitted to a Roman festival, the Great Games, only to be ejected from it, thus infuriating the insulted Volsci into taking up arms.

THE GREAT GAMES

Romans loved their games, and the Great Games (*Magni Ludi* in Latin) were one of the most important state-sponsored festivals in honour of the gods – in this case, Jupiter, king of the gods. They were held in September every year. In earlier years, there was a grand procession to the Circus Maximus, followed by chariot races and theatrical performances (Greek-style tragedies and comedies, adapted for the Roman audience), all of course played out by *plebs* (no member of the elite would stoop so low). Later they were expanded with animal hunts, mock battles and so on. They bore no relation at all to the Greek Olympics.

The *plebs* expressed no interest in fighting over the matter, and attempts were made to treat for peace. No agreement was possible, however, and war looked a certainty until Coriolanus' mother, Veturia, and his wife, Volumnia, were persuaded to enter the Volsci battle line, accompanied by Coriolanus' two little sons, and plead for peace.

It worked. Coriolanus withdrew his army and was never heard of again. The Romans put up a temple to 'Female *Fortuna*' in memory of the event.

Interestingly, Livy tells us that on this occasion the Great Games had to be repeated, though he does not connect this to the Coriolanus affair. One Titus Latinius – presumably a *pleb* – had a dream that the games had not been carried out properly (some flaw or interruption in the correct ritual; Livy is not explicit) and was ordered to inform the consuls. Titus, a shy man – and afraid of being mocked – could not bring himself to do so, and a few days later his son died. Jupiter repeated the order and warned him that there would be an even greater disaster if he did not do as he was told. But still Titus hesitated, before collapsing from a serious illness himself. After he summoned his family to tell them what had happened, they put him on a litter and carried him into the Forum – where he informed the consuls of what he had been told. He instantly recovered and walked home.

486–484 BC: THE BATTLE FOR LAND

In 486 BC a peace treaty was made between Rome and the Hernici clan (map, p. xi), one of the conditions of which granted Rome two-thirds of their territory. The consul Spurius Cassius wanted to give over half of it to the Latins and the rest to the Roman *plebs*, together with parts of state-owned land he claimed were being held in private hands.

The wealthy were not enthusiastic about this, and Livy comments that this was the first attempt to legislate about landholding – which, he notes, always resulted in serious disturbances. We shall see how right he was.

The Senate rejected the whole idea and so did some of the *plebs*, who objected to land being given to the Latins. The other consul, Proculus Verginius, suggested that this was an effort by Spurius Cassius to become popular enough to be made king (always a claim that struck fear into Roman hearts). Cassius then came up with another proposal to win favour – to return to the *plebs* the money they had spent on grain during the recent famine. The *plebs* scornfully rejected this as an effort to buy popularity. When Cassius' term of office ended, he was put on trial and executed for treason.

A FARMER'S LIFE: SETTING AN EXAMPLE

The slave foreman should be older than his men and set an example to them. He should enforce his orders on slaves by what he says, not with the whip. Let him have some property of his own; give him women among his fellow slaves to raise children (this secures loyalty). Free labourers who do outstanding work should be regularly consulted; this wins their dedication to the tasks. Treat him generously – with better rations, occasional days off, allowing him to use your farm to graze his animals – and he will take more interest in his work.

Varro

But the idea of land reform had taken hold among the *plebs*, especially as the spoils of war from the recent battles against the Volsci and Aequi had not been distributed among the troops. They had been sold by the then consul Caeso Fabius and the proceeds put into public funds. As a result, the Volsci and Aequi sensed rebellion in Rome, which they thought could perhaps even result in the *plebs* refusing to fight, so they launched another assault. They were repelled, however.

Although plebeian discontent continued, the senators had worked out how to deal with it. All it needed was one or two tribunes to take the Senate's side to prevent the *plebs* reaching a unanimous decision – an example, perhaps, of tribunes and the wealthier *plebs* deciding to take the senatorial line in their own interests. As a result, senators were still able to recruit the forces they needed to campaign against hostile neighbours.

480 BC: THE ETRUSCANS REPELLED

Nevertheless, there was a feeling among the surrounding peoples of the region that Rome was vulnerable and its military's discipline not what it once was.

The Etruscans observed this, and concluded that it was down to the fact that Rome was being torn apart by political discord – the conflict between rich and poor, that 'poisonous disease of wealthy and powerful communities', as Livy puts it. That was currently being expressed most clearly on the battlefield, with Roman soldiers disobeying their superiors and even deserting their standards. This induced the Etruscans to launch another attack.

The Roman generals, well aware of their own troops' resentments, kept them behind their fortifications and refused to allow them out to fight. The enemy mocked them for their cowardice, which aroused the anger of the troops.

The consuls took full advantage of this by continuing to restrain the men until it became almost impossible to do so, at which point they were unleashed. The Etruscans were not properly deployed and, after a ferocious struggle, the Romans proved victorious.

The consul Quintus Fabius had fought with notable courage, and when the battle was over he made an effort to heal the tension between the Senate and *plebs*: he offered his own houses, as did other Fabii, in which to billet the wounded.

A FARMER'S LIFE: A BAD JOKE

Publius Scipio Nasica, who suppressed many revolutions in the empire, stood as a young man for public office. Looking for votes, he was going around shaking the rough hands of some farm labourers, when he asked one of them, as a joke, whether he spent his time walking on his hands. The word got around, and Scipio was not elected. The country clans felt insulted by this reference to their poverty.

Valerius Maximus

479 BC: THE FABII

Not surprisingly Caeso, a member of the popular Fabius family – supported by the Senate as well as by the *plebs* – was appointed consul next year. In a further effort to unite the Romans, he recommended that the Senate divide up among the *plebs* some of the land that they had won.

He argued that one of the tribunes would probably bring forward the measure anyway, and it would be better if the Senate got ahead of the game: it was right that the men who had won the land with their sweat and blood should have a share of it. But again, nothing came of this proposal.

Rome then suffered a defeat at the hands of its old enemy the Etruscan town of Veii, and, with the Volsci and Aequi uniting and the Sabines up in arms, the Fabii family made an extraordinary offer. They agreed to take on the Veientes themselves, at their own expense, and leave the Romans to deal with everyone else.

The next day, as the 306 members of the Fabii clan drew up in columns and were given the orders to march, cheering crowds accompanied them, praying to the gods for success and the safe return of the heroic band. 'Alas, their prayers were in vain.' After much early success, all perished but one.

But over the next couple of years, despite some close scrapes, the threat to Rome from Veii was finally overcome.

509–473 BC: PLEB POWER – A SUMMARY OF GAINS

- Anyone should have a right to appeal to the *plebs* against any decision made by an official.

- Anyone convicted of planning the return of the monarchy should lose all civil rights.

- The *plebs* should have their own inviolable 'tribunes of the *plebs*', appointed by the Plebeian Assembly.

- The tribunes would be above the law and so have the power to protect the *plebs* as a whole against the consuls.

- They would be able to veto *all* legislation.

- No patrician would be permitted to take the office of tribune.

IV

A NEW
LAW-CODE
AND THE RULE
OF THE TEN:

473-449 BC

473 BC: MURDER OF A TRIBUNE

The demand for the distribution of land was raised again by the tribunes in 474 BC, but the consuls turned it down flat. When their term of office ended, they were arrested by the tribune Genucius, and marched to the court proceedings wearing mourning clothes: their message to both *plebs* and young patricians was that high office simply doomed the bearer to death. Consuls had become nothing but the slaves of the tribunes.

This caused the Senate to convene secret meetings to decide how to handle this dangerous situation. As a result, on the day of the trial, Genucius did not appear. The *plebs* thought that he had been paid off by the Senate, until he was found to be at home, dead.

The *plebs* scattered, and the plebeian tribunes realized that their inviolability meant nothing. Word even got around that the power of the tribunes should be curbed permanently. When the summons to raise troops was issued, the terrified tribunes did nothing to stop it. But the *plebs* were furious. Since the tribunes were useless, they themselves would have to act to try to protect their own interests.

VOLERO COMES TO THE RESCUE

At that moment a man named Volero refused to be enlisted in a lower military rank than that to which he had previously been assigned, i.e. centurion. Arrested, he fought back and appealed to the tribunes, but no one came to help him. So he turned to the *plebs*, calling on them to protect him: 'Why wait for the tribunes? They need *your* help!' Such was the fury of the crowds that the senators retreated into the Senate house. Some wanted to put the *plebs* in their place, but the older members, powerless in the face of the mob and fearing the consequences of conflict, managed to calm the situation.

A FARMER'S LIFE: TRAINING A BULLOCK

To train a young bullock to pull the plough, yoke him to the strongest trained oxen you have, who will restrain him if he pushes forward too fast, and pull him along if he lags. Even better, construct a three-oxen yoke and place the bullock between two veterans. They will prevent him leaping forward, if he halts they will pull him on, and if he lies down, he will be lifted up and dragged on by force.

Columella

At the next election, Volero was appointed as a tribune of the *plebs*. People were afraid he would attempt to make as much trouble for the consuls as possible, but he put the general good above personal grievances and proposed a bill that plebeian officials should always be appointed by the Plebeian (Tribal) Assembly.

This was a significant move, because it prevented the patricians from having any influence on the *plebs'* choice of tribunes.

471 BC: APPIUS CLAUDIUS REBUFFED

The dispute over plebeian power continued, and when Volero was re-elected tribune together with Laetorius, who was a keen supporter of Volero and a soldier of high reputation, the Senate responded by making the feared Appius Claudius (true son of his father) one of the consuls.

Volero continued to argue sanely that the Plebeian (Tribal) Assembly should create plebeian officials, but Laetorius descended to making savage attacks on Appius Claudius as a bully and tyrant. Breaking down mid-speech, Laetorius then told the crowd to meet again the next day when he would get the plebeian appointment measure through or die in the attempt.

On the next day, such chaos ensued between the competing factions that bloodshed was avoided only when the other consul, Quinctius, had Appius Claudius removed from the Forum, calmed down the crowd and told them that the situation would be improved by a period of quiet reflection on the whole matter.

Back in the Senate house, Appius was having none of that. He accused the senators of cowardice and said that they should be supporting him and not the *plebs*. But his was a lone voice and he was forced to give way. The law was passed without opposition, and for the first time the plebeian tribunes were appointed by the Plebeian (Tribal) Assembly.

At the same time, the number of tribunes was increased from two to five.

APPIUS AND QUINCTIUS CONTRASTED

Meanwhile, the Volsci and Aequi, sensing yet another opportunity to take advantage of the split between Senate and *plebs*, laid waste to some Roman territory in the hope that the *plebs* might take action as they had done under Sicinius (p. 71). Appius Claudius was sent against the Volsci, and such was his loathing of the *plebs* and his fury at the defeat over the question of the tribunes that he imposed the most savage discipline upon the troops.

But it made no difference. They simply refused to obey him. Told to march at speed, they slowed down, and, if he urged them to greater effort, they would all immediately slacken off. So he turned his rage on the centurions.

Aware of all this, the Volsci increased the pressure on Appius' troops, who were quite happy to retreat back to camp. But as the rear guard suffered severe casualties and the camp was threatened, the Romans drove the Volsci back.

When Appius attempted to assert his authority, his officers told him it was pointless. The next day he gave orders for the army to move. The Volsci immediately attacked the rear and total chaos ensued. Every man looked to his own safety, until Appius finally managed to halt the retreat. All those who had lost their weapons, standards or other equipment were flogged and beheaded. Of the rest, one in ten were executed ('decimation').

Meanwhile, Quinctius' campaign against the Aequi had gone very differently. The enemy had refused to engage, allowing the Romans to invade their territory and take what they wanted where and when they wanted it. Much valuable material, including cattle, had been seized. All this Quinctius distributed among the troops, while congratulating them on what they had achieved ('which delights soldiers just as much as rewards do'). As a result, his men regarded Quinctius as a father, contrasting him with Appius, the tyrant, and took a more favourable view of the Senate.

470 BC: THE DEATH OF APPIUS CLAUDIUS

The next year saw continued disputes over the distribution of land to the *plebs*. Appius Claudius continued to be its most resolute opponent, as a result of which he was brought to trial by two tribunes.

The Senate continued to support him loyally as the one man determined to assert senatorial power over the *plebs*. Although it was a trial before the *plebs*, Appius did not in any way change his arrogant behaviour, words or looks. His fearlessness so overawed the tribunes and the *plebs* that the trial was adjourned to some date in the future. But before it could resume, he fell ill and died. The tribunes tried to prevent the eulogy in his honour, but the *plebs* insisted on it going ahead: he had been a significant figure and they did not want him 'cheated of the traditional tribute'. Huge numbers attended his funeral.

In 469 BC, smoke from burning farmsteads and the arrival in the city of farmers and their families, fleeing for their lives, alerted the Romans to another assault from the Volsci and Aequi. This put a stop to the threat of violence from the *plebs* over the redistribution of land, and two years of conflict ensued. It became a war of attrition and they eventually broke the enemies' will to continue.

467 BC: ROOM FOR EVERYONE

The new consul Titus Aemilius proposed to make grants of land to plebeian families. This was eagerly accepted by the tribunes, but since the owners of the land were mostly patrician it required a compromise put together by the other consul, Quintus Fabius, to win acceptance. He pointed out that Rome had recently commandeered, from the Volsci, much land in the pleasant region of Antium on the coast. Why not give the *plebs* that?

This solved the problem, but because there was plenty for everyone, and 'human nature being what it is', many *plebs* rejected the idea of being so far removed from the security of proximity to Rome. The Romans therefore had to bring local Volscians into the scheme to bring the new settlement up to a viable size.

462 BC: A NEW LEGAL CODE?

Rome was struck with a plague at the same time as it had to face more dangerous attacks from the Volsci and the Aequi. Once they had dealt with the plague, the *plebs* – as Livy regularly comments – could turn to their own interests again.

The tribune Terentilius, taking advantage of the absence of the consuls in the battle line, argued that their power was more oppressive than even that of the kings, and that it was time it was restrained. He proposed a formal codification of the law, which would limit and define the powers of consuls in such a way that they could not simply do whatever they felt like.

A FARMER'S LIFE: LOSING THE FARM

An ancient Greek author described chatting with someone he had met who lived in an extended family group, each with sons and daughters. They survived by hunting and working their small plot as tenants (they had not inherited or bought it). The fathers, although free men, were pretty poor and worked as hired labourers, looking after the cattle of a wealthy landowner. When he died, the fathers' property was confiscated, as were their own few cattle. But they still had their calves, and sufficient land for grazing them, with some hay put by to see them through the winter. When summer came, they drove them into the mountains, where there was plenty of water, no cattle pests, gorgeous meadows and lush vegetation.

Note: This kind of movement is called 'transhumance'. It must have been very common, but it is rarely mentioned in ancient literature.

This was fiercely contested by the patricians, who argued that consuls were already subject to the law – all this proposal would achieve was yet again to upset the even balance of power between the Senate and the people – and they appealed to the other (richer?) tribunes to hold things up until the consuls had returned from the battlefield. This was agreed, and the achievements of the consuls in the recent war were celebrated.

461 BC: THE DEBATE DEADLOCKED

But the issue would not go away, and this time *all* the tribunes supported Terentilius. Proceedings were not helped by a number of very ominous portents: an earthquake, a talking cow and raining lumps of meat. The Sibylline Books were duly consulted and revealed that foreigners were about to cause trouble, and political factions should be avoided. The tribunes dismissed this as an invention designed to prevent the discussion of the proposal.

THE SIBYLLINE BOOKS

The Sybil was a prophetess from Cumae (near Naples). She offered King Tarquinius Priscus (p. 38) nine sacred books for 300 gold coins. Rejected, she burned three and offered the remaining six for the same price. Rejected again, she burned three more, and offered the final three at the same price again. Priscus gave up and bought them. These books did not actually foretell the future but gave accurate instructions on how to placate the gods if the omens looked bad. They were lost to fire in 83 BC, but the Senate ordered a commission of three to hunt the Mediterranean for a new set. Christians destroyed them c. AD 400.

At that point it was announced that the Volsci and Aequi were on the march yet again. The tribunes denounced this as an obviously baseless scare-story, designed by the Senate to get the *plebs* out of the city with a view to taking revenge on the tribunes. They urged the *plebs* not to exchange their civilian gear for uniforms and allow themselves to be tricked like this into slavery. The military levy went ahead, a riot ensued, and every arrest of a citizen refusing to sign up was challenged by the tribunes. It was chaos. Caeso Quinctius, a hot-headed senator, attempted to take on the tribunes, but the tribune Verginius stood up to him. This only encouraged Caeso to lose his rag completely and leave himself open to serious charges.

Caeso's father was the patrician Cincinnatus (in Latin, 'with hair in ringlets'), and he pleaded with the people to forgive his son's extravagant behaviour. An ex-tribune, Marcus Fictor, then revealed that – during a drunken punch-up in the Subura – Caeso had knocked out his brother and killed him, but Marcus had never been able to get legal satisfaction for this crime.

THE SUBURA

This was the low-life area of Rome, divided from the important Forum area – which was full of monuments – by a magnificent wall (that still stands today). This was a precautionary move: the Subura was a place that often caught fire.

KILLING WITH KINDNESS

This made for a complex legal situation. But it was finally resolved when Caeso went into voluntary exile in Etruria, and his father sold everything to pay a huge fine, which left him penniless and 'living in a deserted hovel across the Tiber like a banished man'.

Terentilius' proposed codification of the law, however, was successfully put on hold, mainly because the younger senators, while continuing to resist it, otherwise bent over backwards to strike up friendly relations with the tribunes and the *plebs*. This enabled the *plebs* to pass various pieces of legislation without any problems. An uneasy political peace then ruled.

460–451 BC: YEARS OF CHAOS

Around 460 BC, a group of exiles and slaves, led by the Sabine Herdonius, seized the Capitoline ridge, but the town of Tusculum came to Rome's rescue and the coup was foiled. The Aequi and the Sabines threatened Rome, and Cincinnatus was called from his plough by the Senate to become dictator (p. 50), as a temporary measure, to save the day. This he duly did, famously returning to his plough afterwards. Further attacks by the Aequi and attempts by the Senate to raise troops were hindered (as ever) by the tribunes' efforts to get Terentilius' code of law agreed, but in 457 BC the Senate did grant a concession – or was it a sweetener? – that the tribunes' numbers should be increased from five to ten.

There was a further concession too: it was agreed some land around the Aventine ridge be assigned to plebeians by drawing lots.

451–450 BC: THE RULE OF THE TEN

By now it had become clear even to the tribunes that they needed a different strategy if the law was to be codified. They suggested that a board of legislators should be appointed, consisting of senators and *plebs*, to investigate the whole question of a new code of law.

Three representatives were sent to Athens to investigate the famous laws of the Athenian statesman Solon and in general to examine the political institutions of various Greek city-states. On the strength of their findings, a board of ten was invited to produce a written code of Roman law.

As a result, after the rule of the kings, and then of the Senate and consuls, came the rule of the ten decemvirs (Latin *decem*, 'ten', compare 'decimal'; *vir*, 'man', compare 'virile').

The code turned out to be a tremendous success, delivering prompt justice enjoyed by the highest and lowest in the state. Further, it was made clear that, while the finest legal minds in Rome had been at work on the code, there was always room for improvement, and, as a result of enthusiastic public engagement with the whole process, various amendments were introduced. Livy comments in his history that the whole initiative 'equalized the rights of all, both the highest and the lowest'.

But at the same time, it became obvious that more needed to be done, and it was decided to add two more codes to the existing ten. A new committee of decemvirs was elected to oversee this task. It was at this point that serious trouble began.

WHO RULES?

The son of Appius Claudius, true to form, managed to work himself into the presidency of this new committee and proceeded to ensure that his own candidates were appointed.

When the ten decemvirs paraded before the people, each of them was accompanied by twelve attendants (lictors), carrying the dreaded *fasces* (p. 21). This was tyranny – a powerless Senate, no more consuls or tribunes, no more right of appeal, no help for anyone wrongly accused. And to cap it all, the decemvirs agreed among themselves that no one would argue with one another's decisions. It soon became clear that Appius Claudius had the *plebs* as his target: there were to be no more political concessions. This was as unpopular with the Senate as it was with the *plebs*.

Still, when the two new legal codes were completed, the job of the decemvirs would be done and it was assumed that Rome would revert to republican rule. But when election day arrived, no new officials were nominated, and the Ten paraded with their lictors as before.

ROME AT BAY

It had not escaped the notice of Rome's enemies that the city was now hopelessly divided. The Sabines invaded, farms were ransacked and burned down, and refugees flooded into the city. The Aequi were also mustering for an attack.

It had been so long since the Roman Senate had been summoned that there were no senators about; they had all departed for their country retreats. The *plebs* were refusing to enlist. A meeting was called and a few senators turned up – including Marcus Horatius Barbatus, who denounced the Ten and said the real battle was not with Rome's external enemies, but with the decemvirs. He called them the 'ten Tarquins'. Not that there was anything in principle wrong with the kings, he said, except their violence and pride. And if that was intolerable in kings, who would endure it in men who held no *legal* office at all? The Ten had better beware: if they forbade free speech in the Senate, tongues would soon be wagging in the streets:

> The self-seeking and greed of tyrants are no match for honest indignation fighting to throw off its chains. The real war which the people of Rome must fight is a war against those who, appointed to office in order to give us laws, have left our country at the mercy of their own whims; it is against those who abolished free elections and annual offices, which are the sole guarantee of liberty for all, who, without any mandate from the people, exercise the power of Kings. Whom do you support? The people? You've done nothing for them! The elite? But the Senate has not met for a year, and now that we are met, we are forbidden to discuss the situation. Do not, I warn you, trust that the people will fear the consequences of rebelling. What we are enduring now is worse than anything we may fear in the future.

Much more in this vein followed, but no conclusion was reached. But at least the motion to raise troops was accepted. The results were catastrophic, however, as the troops had no interest in fighting under the orders of the decemvirs. So Rome went into full defensive mode: all men of military age were ordered to be on guard duty.

Meanwhile, in operations on Sabine territory, one Lucius Siccius began urging the soldiers not to fight but to demand the election of tribunes, who had been made powerless during the rule of the decemvirs. He was secretly murdered. The decemvirs, realizing that this was a step too far, gave him a hero's military funeral at public cost. It made little difference to the *plebs'* feelings about them.

ANOTHER LUCRETIA?

Even worse was to follow. Appius Claudius was determined to have his way with a beautiful young girl, Verginia, daughter of a highly respected Roman centurion, Lucius Verginius. Appius ordered a dependant of his, Marcus Claudius, to claim that she was a slave and arrest her as she was going to school.

ROMAN SCHOOLS

Anyone in the Roman world could set up a school as long as he had suitable premises – a shop, a house, a tent, a stoa (a pillared colonnade, giving protection from sun and rain). But education was the sphere of the elite males, who had the leisure to indulge in it, unlike the *plebs*. It was designed to train them in the art of public speaking, and so give them the ability to win arguments in the law courts and the Senate. Livy invented the school in his account of Appius Claudius and Verginia; girls were educated at home.

This was greeted with outrage, but she was brought before the court, where Marcus said he had excellent evidence that proved she was a slave. Appius, who had put himself in charge of the court, ruled that her father should be called back from military service – after all, Verginia was subject to her father – and in the meantime the girl should be kept in Marcus' custody.

At that point, Verginia's fiancé, Icilius, arrived, saying he would do everything in his power to protect his wife-to-be. Appius agreed to release her for one day, and Icilius sent friends at speed to alert Verginius to the situation. Well aware of what was happening, Appius attempted to get a message through to have Verginius arrested, but it was too late.

The next day, Verginius and his daughter arrived at the Forum in mourning garb, and he and Icilius went about the sympathetic, weeping crowd, pleading for their support. Appius paid no attention whatsoever, but as a horrified Livy reports: 'There and then Appius gave judgement for Marcus and declared Verginia to be his slave.' This was greeted with incredulity. Verginius threatened force, but Appius commanded his lictors to clear the rebellious crowd so that Marcus could take charge of his slave.

Verginius stood there, helpless, but then asked if he could consult his family nurse privately, to find out if he really was Verginia's father. Appius agreed, and Verginius moved the nurse and his daughter aside to the shops next to the shrine of Cloacina – where, snatching a knife from a butcher, he cried, 'My daughter, this is the only way to make you free!' and stabbed her in the heart. Then, turning to Appius, he exclaimed, 'May the curse of this blood rest upon your head forever!' and made his escape through the crowd.

A riot broke out, but the well-liked Lucius Valerius, son of a consul, and consul Marcus Horatius Barbatus took charge and ordered the lictors to refuse to obey Appius because he had no official rank. Appius fled in fear of his life.

BACK TO THE SACRED MOUNT

Verginius raced back to the army, where he told the whole story, including the flight of Appius. The decemvirs' attempts to assert their authority failed and the whole army marched to Rome, where they urged the *plebs* to recover their freedom and restore the tribunes. The final result was that the army and the whole military and civilian population decamped to the Sacred Mount in protest, leaving Rome empty except for the Senate, now sitting in complete solitude in the Forum.

The Senate's political attacks on the decemvirs were so ferocious that they were forced to bow to the weight of opinion, give up their power and yield to the Senate's authority. Valerius and Horatius were promptly sent to the Sacred Mount to agree terms for the return of the population to Rome. The *plebs* made it clear that all they wanted was an equitable settlement, i.e. the tribunate restored, together with the right of appeal, and no punishment of those responsible for urging the army and the people to win back their freedoms. They did, however, also express a wish for the decemvirs to surrender and threatened to burn them alive.

449 BC: PLEB POWER INCREASED

Without delay, the *plebs* and army left the Sacred Mount for Rome, where the demands of the *plebs* were met in full and new tribunes were elected. Valerius and Horatius were appointed consuls. Further, it was agreed that:

- Any resolution passed by the *plebs* should be binding upon the *whole* people (proposed, but not enacted).

- The right of appeal should be widened and guaranteed.

- The sacrosanctity of the tribunes should be restored.

Since political liberty had now been reinstated, the tribunes brought charges against the decemvirs. Appius Claudius, accused of having 'no part in the mutual compact of civilized men', was inevitably found guilty, but used the right of appeal – which he had denied to so many others – and was consigned to prison to await a formal trial. When all his appeals for pity failed, he killed himself. In fact, all those who conspired against Verginia met their end.

Meanwhile, the Twelve Tables – the original ten laws, plus the later two – were inscribed in bronze and permanently exhibited for all to read, as were all future laws. No longer were laws 'suppressed or falsified by the consuls to suit their own convenience'.

RECONCILIATION?

It was inevitable that the patricians would find the restoration of plebeian rights difficult to take, especially as the two consuls, Valerius and Horatius, had proved to be such enthusiastic supporters of the *plebs*. But the tribune Duilius took upon himself the responsibility of assuring them that the tribunes had no intention of raking up all the old problems, which had now been solved, and that the tribunes would act strictly in accordance with the law in all their political dealings.

PLEB POWER: A SUMMARY OF GAINS

507 BC: The *plebs* won the right to appeal against arrest.

494 BC: Two sacrosanct tribunes of the *plebs* were to be annually appointed by a people's assembly.

471 BC: The tribunes were now appointed by the Plebeian Assembly, so that the patricians had no say. The number of tribunes was raised from two to five.

457 BC: The number of tribunes was raised to ten.

451–450 BC: The Twelve Tables were inscribed in bronze and exhibited for all to read, as all future laws would be.

449 BC: It was decided that the right of appeal should be widened and guaranteed; the sacrosanctity of the tribunes should be restored; a very dangerous Sabine assault was foiled. The Senate refused a triumph. But the *plebs* unanimously voted for it and for the first time it was celebrated without Senatorial authorization.

V

FURTHER PLEBEIAN SUCCESS AND THE EMERGENCE OF CAMILLUS:

449–390 BC

FOREIGN AFFAIRS

Rome's internal problems had been the subject of much interest, as ever, to the surrounding clans. The Latins and the Hernici remained loyal allies, and sent their congratulations on the recent reconciliation. Not so the Volsci, the Aequi and the Sabines, always on the lookout for weakness in this powerful state. But thanks to the new political settlement, this time Rome had no problem in raising troops, both young and old, to take to the field, and, when they found themselves in a spot of bother against the Aequi, it simply took the consul Valerius reminding the *plebs* that the decemvirs and Appius were no longer in charge of affairs.

Livy found ringing words to end Valerius' appeal: 'Prove today that the heart of a Roman soldier is what it always was before the decemvirs came to their accursed power, and that a Roman's courage is none the less for his equality before the law!' Valerius' victory spurred on Horatius against the Sabines, who proved stern foes, but the Romans eventually came out on top, and the enemy fled, leaving their camp to be plundered at will.

After all their recent internal troubles, the Romans were overjoyed at this double success and the tribunes demanded that the two consuls should be given the public honour of a triumph (p. 155). The senators objected to this on the grounds that it was their job to make the decision, not the *plebs'*. But the public vote was overwhelming, and the triumph was celebrated at the bidding of the *plebs*.

448–447 BC: UNEASY CALM

With the end of control by the decemvirs, elections were held for tribunes and consuls. Five of the previous tribunes wanted to be re-elected, but that was against the law. As a result, it was decided for the first time to co-opt patricians as tribunes to make up the numbers. This caused a degree of resentment in one of the tribunes, who over the course of the year was given the nickname 'Prickly'. The next year's consuls maintained not just internal but also external peace, though the tensions between patricians and *plebs* continued.

Livy far-sightedly summarized the situation as follows: 'True moderation in the defence of political liberties is very difficult to achieve: everyone claims to want equality but makes every effort to come out on top. Our anxiety to avoid domination leads us to practise it ourselves; the injustice we fight, we visit on others, as if the only available choice were to inflict wrong or suffer it.'

446 BC: THE ROMANS RALLY

And Livy was right: the following year, the old tensions reared their heads and troops could not be raised. This sent the inevitable signal to the leaders of the Volsci and the Aequi to combine forces with a devastating attack on Latium, from which they returned with much booty and without a response from the Roman army.

The fourth-time consul Titus Quinctius called a mass meeting and blasted the Roman people, stating that their trust in communal life had been poisoned by political discord and party strife, with the *plebs* in a state of permanent conflict in their desire for liberty and the patricians lusting for power, each side loathing the other's official representatives.

Quinctius invited the *plebs* to consider what had just happened to them: the enemy had destroyed their farms and come within a short distance of Rome without response. Whose interests had been served by that? Could tribunes restore their losses? They could stick to their petty politics if they wanted to, he said, but 'we shall soon be fighting in the streets of Rome and the Volsci will be climbing the Capitol – unless you give me the chance to take revenge upon these marauders, capture their camp and remove the threat from Rome!'

This magnificent speech was greeted with acclaim, troops were raised, and in three days they were in striking distance of the enemy; their victory was soon complete.

445 BC: SOCIAL MIXED MARRIAGE?

With the republican system restored, the tribune Canuleius at once put forward two controversial proposals: the first was to permit marriage between patricians and plebeians, and the second to allow one of the two consuls to be a plebeian. Both proposals were inevitably contested by the Senate.

The first, it was claimed, would contaminate the blood of ancient noble families – what child would know from which stock he really came? It would also threaten the ancient privilege of patrician families to take the auspices in order to reveal the will of the gods.

As for the second, if it was possible for one consul to be a plebeian, it followed there would soon be a demand for both consuls to be plebeian. Further, the most likely plebeians to be placed in that position would be the rabble-rousers – the sort that always refused to allow the levy of troops unless their proposals were passed, 'as they are doing now, while we are being threatened by old enemies like the Volsci, Aequi and Veii'.

But Canuleius gave the Senate a history lesson, pointing out that none of the kings had been Romans, that Rome had always been happy to welcome in immigrants who could become senators and consuls, and that Rome had changed radically since its foundation – new priesthoods, new powers, new offices, and so on. How many of the senators sitting in front of him had originally been from an Alban or Sabine family – not noble birth at all?

As for mixed marriages, it had always been the privilege of families alone to make their own choice about those with whom to create an alliance. Did they want to turn Rome into two separate communities? Why not propose a ban on marriage between rich and poor?

'I wonder you do not pass a law to stop a plebeian living next door to a nobleman, or walking in the same street, or going to the same party, or standing side by side with him in the Forum,' he went on. To whom did the ultimate authority of the state belong: the Senate or the Roman people? Why did the people finish with the monarchy? Was it to give supreme authority to the Senate, or to achieve liberty for all?

The controversy raged on, but the Senate eventually yielded on the question of mixed marriage, hoping that the grateful *plebs* would forget about appointing consuls from among their own.

In the end, a compromise was reached. It was agreed to appoint at least three military tribunes (senior military officers; the number would vary from three to six) with *consular* authority, from both patricians and *plebs* alike, *in place of the consuls*. The question of the consuls was left up in the air (they continued to appear from time to time).

In fact, the three candidates returned were all patricians. As Livy comments, 'The fact that plebeians had been *allowed* to stand was enough to satisfy the *plebs*. Such decency of feeling, such fairness and magnanimity characterized, on that occasion, the whole body of the Roman *plebs*. Where would you find it today in one single man?'

443 BC: CENSORS

The job of the censors was to classify the people's status in accordance with their property and so define their role in the military, capacity to pay taxes and so on (p. 45). But the census had lapsed for many years and needed to be restored. This was clearly an enormous and very tiresome task, and the Senate decided it needed an official of its own, with its own staff, to ensure that the job was done and the records were safely kept.

This was an extremely important development because, knowing of Rome's finances in detail, the censors alone could judge which projects were viable and which not.

439 BC: EXPLOITING A FAMINE

When a very serious famine hit Rome – some said it was a bad harvest, others that it was the pleasures of city life and the turmoil of the political situation that had called the *plebs* away from their farms – Lucius Minucius was appointed controller of supplies to purchase grain from wherever he could.

Having failed almost completely in that respect, he forced people to sell their stocks if they had a surplus, cut the slaves' rations, and much else, but all that did was reveal how disastrous the situation was. Many of the poorest gave up and committed suicide.

Spurius Maelius, an extremely wealthy man, decided it was time to intervene. He purchased vast quantities of grain from Etruria, which he then distributed for free among the poor. This made him very popular, and he began to nurture political ambitions, some said, to restore the monarchy with himself as king.

Minucius meanwhile continued his work as controller of supplies, but in the process found evidence that Spurius was building up a store of arms in his house and talking to various people about the possibility of revolution. The Senate decided that the situation was so serious that it was necessary to appoint a dictator, and they turned to the now very aged Cincinnatus (p. 92) to repeat his role of many years before.

He placed a picket around the city and summoned the people to an assembly. There he called upon his sidekick Servilius to instruct Spurius to present himself before the dictator. Spurius fled, calling upon the people to save him, but he was cut down. Cincinnatus then addressed the crowd, who were in some degree of turmoil, explaining why this had happened and accusing Spurius of imagining that he could buy power in Rome and reduce the Roman *plebs* to servitude by tossing them a biscuit.

426 BC: ENCOURAGING THE PLEBS TO UP THEIR GAME

After summoning a dictator Mamercus Aemilius to defeat a dangerous attack from the Etruscan settlements of Veii and Fidenae – dictators could be appointed whenever danger of any sort threatened – the generals staged a fabulous celebratory games, much enjoyed by both the Romans and their neighbours – who were impressed by the courtesy with which they were treated.

The tribunes, however, used this to attack the *plebs*. Why did they admire their political rivals (i.e. the military top brass) so much? Why did they remain enslaved to them, and not vote for plebeians to become military tribunes? 'Aspiration must have something to aspire to,' the *plebs* were lectured. It was high time they insisted they were just as good as anyone else.

As a result, more plebeian candidates put themselves forward, proposing measures such as land distribution, establishing new settlements, and taxing the wealthy who owned most of the public land.

417 BC: FOILING THE TRIBUNES

Two tribunes decided to demand that all the land that had been acquired by force of arms (as opposed to inherited) should be distributed among the *plebs*. Since virtually all of it had been obtained by the nobility long ago, the senators were in a quandary about how to respond.

Then the grandson of the hated decemvir Appius Claudius suggested that some of the senators do what his grandfather had: approach those tribunes who were new to the game and just wanted to curry favour with the wealthy – and who had *not* had that land redistribution idea – and point out that they had been left out in the cold by this initiative. Why did they not ingratiate themselves to the senators – especially the leading senators – and win their favour by trying to block it?

Six tribunes agreed. When the proposal for the redistribution of land was put to the people, the senators invited everyone to come to the rescue of the country and reject such a subversion of the natural order of things. The result? With the help of those tribunes, the resolution was not passed, despite the insults and abuse they received from their colleagues.

This was yet more evidence of the collusion between the Senate and the wealthier *plebs*.

414 BC: WHO OWNS THE LAND?

The military tribune Postumius was given command against the Aequi and soon forced his way into the town of Bolae, but then broke his promise to allow his men to keep the plunder. When he got back to Rome, he argued against a proposal that land should be given to the soldiers who had conquered it, and remarked, 'If my men don't keep their mouths shut on that matter, they had better look out for themselves.'

This did not go down well, and he was accused of treating his men like slaves – even threatening to punish them. A riot broke out, and efforts to quell it failed. Postumius was recalled and started handing out savage punishments. He was eventually stoned to death by his own men. An inquiry into the events was vetoed by the tribunes.

But the *plebs'* frustration continued, not only because the elites had held on to their own land by force, but also because they refused to distribute even recently acquired land, which the *plebs* knew full well would eventually fall into the hands of the rich.

406 BC: A VITAL CONCESSION

Because Veii had insultingly told a Roman mission that had come to declare war on the town to take a running jump, Rome demanded reparations. This was refused, and the Senate demanded that war be declared, but the tribunes resisted, claiming that the Senate seemed keener on fighting the Roman *plebs* than anyone else; they were keeping their own citizens engaged in foreign battles when they could be quietly at home, dreaming of forbidden hopes – liberty, a farm of their own to cultivate, the distribution of public land, and voting as they wanted to. The tribunes persuaded some old campaigners to put in an appearance. They counted up the years of their service, pointed to their wounds and scars, and wondered if they really had any more blood to give for their country. The Senate dropped its demand.

Nonetheless, a force *was* sent against the Volsci, which was very successful. Further, instead of committing mass slaughter, the soldiers were told to put down their arms and take prisoners – 2,500 in all. When the general in charge had called in all the units that had been engaged in the battle, they were allowed to sack the town of Anxur, which was rich from a long period of prosperity. This immediately improved relations between the *plebs* and the patricians in Rome, and the Senate, without prompting from anyone else, issued a decree that soldiers would from now on *be paid out of public funds*. Up until then, no soldier had been paid for his service; it was his civic duty to serve, according to his ability to arm himself (p. 46). Sometimes booty was allotted after a successful battle (or he took it for himself); and doubtless local grandees helped out soldiers financially where necessary, local pride being at stake.

This lifesaver for the families of the poorer *plebs* was greeted with tremendous celebrations. But inevitably the tribunes, seeing it as a move by the Senate to win the favour of the *plebs*, took against it. Where was the money to come from? A tax on the people? What about long-retired soldiers?

But the patricians were the first to pay the new tax, and, because silver coinage had not yet been invented, their wagons heaped with bronze bars lumbering towards the treasury made an impressive sight. This persuaded the wealthy plebeians 'of leading rank and friends of the elite' to do the same, and their example persuaded every *pleb* to pay up, according to their census-determined status (p. 45).

402 BC: MILITARY WINTER QUARTERS

The powerful town of Veii had appointed a king, against the wishes of the other Etruscan communities, and as a result was preparing to take on the Romans on their own. The Romans then took the unprecedented step of establishing *winter* quarters (p. 2) and laying siege to the town; prior to this, winter had always been a time for rest and recovery. This aroused the ire of the tribunes, who accused the Senate of engaging in politics by removing from Rome a substantial portion of the plebeian voters; they were effectively enslaving – and compromising yet further the liberty and freedom of – the ordinary people.

Appius Claudius was invited to put the tribunes in their place. He argued that they were like dishonest traders looking for work:

their one aim in life seemed to be finding something wrong in the political situation so that they could be asked to put it right. They were rather like masters of families who absolutely refused to allow anyone else to make any suggestions about how they should treat their slaves. All the tribunes wanted to do was stop any productive cooperation between patricians and *plebs*.

Appius pointed out that soldiers were now being *paid*: that was fair, but surely a year's pay should produce a year's work? The soldiers were citizens, not mercenaries! Besides, Veii was now surrounded, its farms neglected, its cultivated land ruined. Was now really the time to retreat?

And consider the work the soldiers had already put in, surrounding Veii with ramparts, trenches, forts, earthworks, towers and so on. Should Rome abandon all that, just to have to start it again the next summer?

On top of that, he stressed, the soldiers must learn to be patient. They should take the long view of what was required for victory in these circumstances, just like hunters in the woods and mountains, tracking their prey whatever the weather. Their enemies must learn that, once the Roman army had laid siege to a city, there would be no going back.

The men of Rome must not allow the tribunes to sow dissension among the *plebs*, and let that dissension spread among the army. Or was it the case that liberty in Rome now meant no respect for the Senate and its officials, or for Rome's laws, ancestral customs, their fathers' institutions or military discipline?

This powerful speech won the day, and the war against Veii went ahead, but other cities joined Veii, fearing what would happen to them if Veii were defeated. The bitter fighting ground on – and off – for some ten years, until Veii fell to a strategy devised by the great Roman general Camillus. He opened up access for his troops right into the middle of the city, by tunnelling under and into it. In this way, Veii finally fell.

392 BC: DIVIDING UP THE PLUNDER

Veii was a fabulously rich city, and Camillus was aware that the plunder would be greater than that from all previous campaigns put together. So he wrote to the Senate to ask them what he should do about it.

The old senator Licinius proposed that any willing Roman could go to Veii and claim a share of it. This was opposed by Appius Claudius, who said that plunder should go into the public treasury to pay the troops, because every family would feel the benefit; idlers in Rome should not be allowed to get their hands on booty won by soldiers fighting for their country.

Licinius replied that a gift should be made of it to the *plebs* in return for everything they had put up with over the past ten years. The *plebs* were already being bled white with taxation; this war had taken the best years of their life; and what a man had won and taken home with his own hands was far more satisfying than a handout. This was finally agreed, since it would put the Senate on the side of the *plebs*, and thousands of Romans left for Veii to take advantage of it.

OMENS

When the fighting was over in Veii, Camillus found that the booty was vastly more than even he had expected and he prayed that, if his luck seemed excessive to the gods, he would be able to make up for it with the least hurt to himself or to Rome. But as he turned round, he tripped over, and this was seen as a sign that his wish would not be fulfilled.

Further, since the victory after such a length of time seemed like a gift from heaven, women crowded into the temples to thank the gods, while the Senate decreed a four-day victory celebration. Camillus rode into Rome on a chariot drawn by four white horses in a triumph on a scale never seen before, which seemed to make him something of a godlike figure and, some thought, was dangerously over the top for a mere human being. Two years later, Rome paid the devastating price.

TRANSFERRING A GOD

Among the goods that were transferred from Veii to Rome was the famous statue of the goddess Juno, wife of Jupiter, king of the gods. This was a job that required enormous care, and young soldiers, washed and dressed in white – and treating the whole operation with the greatest reverence – could hardly bring themselves to lay their hands on the statue, which Etruscan religion permitted only very few priests even to touch.

Then one of the soldiers asked, 'Juno, do you *want* to go to Rome?' The soldiers all confirmed that she nodded her head in agreement. Further, it required minimal power to remove her from her place, and she was so easy to transport that it seemed as if she was coming of her own free will. Undamaged, she was taken to the place reserved for her on the Aventine, where the temple dedicated to her by Camillus was built.

THE WOMEN'S GIFT TO APOLLO

Camillus had agreed to dedicate one-tenth of the plunder from Veii to the god Apollo. That presented a problem: it had already been divided up among the Roman people. It was decided that the people should calculate the value of the plunder they had taken and pay one-tenth of it into the treasury.

This did not endear Camillus to the *plebs*. However, he pointed out that the property of Veii surely included the *land*, and one-tenth of the value of *that* could be paid into the treasury, presumably by those who bought it. The money thus withdrawn was used to buy gold, to be turned into a mixing bowl for Apollo at Delphi.

Unfortunately, not enough gold could be found! But the (wealthy elite) women of Rome solved the problem by offering all their gold ornaments to be melted down. They were rewarded by being allowed to drive around in four-wheeled carriages during games and festivals, and in ordinary carriages at other times.

C. 390 BC: A SECOND ROME?

In an attempt to settle the *plebs'* demand for land, the government proposed offering two acres each to 3,000 *plebs* willing to settle in territory captured from the Volsci. But it was pointed out that much richer and better-cultivated land was available in Veii. So why not send half the *plebs* and half the Roman Senate there and set up a substate of Rome?

The patricians would have none of it: if *plebs* and patricians were in constant conflict in Rome, the same would happen in Veii. And what if captured Veii became even more powerful under Romans than it had been before? With some (wealthy?) plebeian tribunes joining the senators in opposing it, the idea was dropped – but it would not go away.

It was Camillus who moved the dial on the argument by saying that he would like nothing more than to see the town he had captured thronging with people, to remind him of what he had achieved. On the other hand, surely it was clear that Veii's defeat proved the gods had abandoned the town, and it would be quite wrong to see it repopulated.

When the proposal was again put to the people, it was defeated not by threats or by force, but by appeals to the *plebs* not to desert Rome – their native city with its gods and all its holy places – nor to be driven into exile to a city that had been its bitter enemy. What Roman would ever want to live on captive soil, or exchange victorious Rome for vanquished Veii?

Thus the proposal was defeated, and the Senate was so pleased with the result that it granted every plebeian three and a half acres of land from Veii's surrounding territory.

THE SCHOOLMASTER OF FALERII

Camillus was then sent to deal with the town of Falerii, which had supported Veii. Since its army refused to engage in open combat, Camillus ravaged its territory and siege operations began.

As it so happened, the schoolmaster of the children from the most important families of the town used to take them for a walk every day for play and exercise. One day, he walked them straight into the Roman camp and, presumably in the hope of a reward, offered them to Camillus, pointing out who they were and saying that the town was now at his mercy.

Camillus accused him of an outrageous act of treachery, telling him that war had its laws, as peace did, and Romans fought their wars with respect for the common bonds of humanity: they had come to fight men, not children. The schoolmaster was stripped naked and had his hands tied, and the children were given sticks with which to beat him back into the town.

The result was that the people of Falerii immediately sued for peace. They sent an embassy to Camillus, saying that his honourable behaviour had persuaded them that they would live better under Rome than under their own government. They told him that the gates of the city were open, and arms and hostages were there to be taken. Falerii was also punished with a fine to cover the cost of the Roman army's pay for a year, which relieved Rome's people of the war tax.

PLEB POWER: A SUMMARY OF GAINS

449 BC: The *plebs* could demand that a triumph be celebrated.

448 BC: Patricians were co-opted as plebeian tribunes; the consuls were replaced by 3–6 'military tribunes' with consular authority, from both patricians and *plebs* alike (in the event, consuls did pop up now and again).

445 BC: Mixed marriage between patricians and *plebs* was made legal.

VI

THE COMING OF
THE GAULS AND
DESTRUCTION
OF ROME:

390–350 BC

At this time, a *pleb* named Caedicius told an official that he had heard a voice at night instructing him to inform the officials that the Gauls were coming. This was brushed aside. At the same time Camillus, who had been in mourning for his son, was charged with mishandling the plunder from Veii. He consulted his friends and allies and made the decision to go into exile, expressing the hope that, if he had been wrongly accused, the gods should punish Rome. And they did.

Wave upon wave of Gauls began crossing the Alps to look for land in which to settle. Rumour had it that this outlandish collection of warriors with their bizarre weapons had already defeated several Etruscan legions by the time they camped outside the city of Clusium, which immediately asked Rome for help.

Rome sent an embassy, and the Gauls made their demand: they wanted land and, if they did not get it, they would fight for it. The Romans asked what justice there was in that – and what were the Gauls doing in Etruria anyway? – to which the answer came that 'all things belonged to the brave who carried justice on the point of their swords'. The Roman embassy agreed with them, drew their swords and massacred the envoys. But that was a dreadful crime, completely against the law of nations. It meant war.

A Roman army was quickly assembled, but it was hopelessly outnumbered, disorganized and tactically out-thought by the Gallic leader Brennus. Half of the army fled behind the security of the walls of Veii; the other half fled back to Rome, pursued by the Gauls, and took refuge in the Citadel, a defensible spur of the Capitoline ridge.

390 BC: ABANDONING ROME:
A PLEB TO THE RESCUE

The situation was desperate. It was decided that the younger soldiers, with their wives and children, should join those in the Citadel – where food and weapons had been gathered – and that the Vestal Virgins should remove all the sacred objects and take them to safety, far away from Rome. Those who could flee should do so, and the old should be left to their fate, in which the Senate agreed to share (Latin *senatus* derives from *senex*, 'old man', compare 'senile'). The Vestal Virgins buried in the ground what they could not carry, divvied up everything else between them, and made for the bridge over the Tiber.

A *pleb*, Lucius Albinus, seeing the Vestals struggling along with Rome's most sacred objects, told his wife and children to step down from the cart in which he was taking them to safety and allow the Vestals and their sacred property on board. In that way, they all made their escape.

VESTAL VIRGINS

Vesta was the goddess of the hearth, the centre of the home, and was located in a specially built sanctuary where burned the sacred, eternal fire (cf. Swan Vesta matches) – the symbol of Rome's permanence. The Vestal Virgins – chosen from the age of six – had to tend it and ensure it never went out. In 420 BC, one Vestal, Postumia, was put on trial for a sexual offence, but, as it emerged, quite wrongly: all she had done was dress rather well and talk rather more freely and amusingly than a woman in her position should.

One other duty of the Vestals was to look after the *fascinum* (basic meaning 'evil spell, bewitchment', root of our 'fascinating'), i.e. an erect phallus – or, just to be clear, a huge model of one. It was supposed to avert evil. The Vestals lived in a considerable degree of comfort and were allowed to drive around in carriages. They were deeply respected.

THE FATE OF THE ELITE

Although some sources say that Servius surrounded Rome with a protective stone wall, that is not the case. If it had been, the Gauls would never have got past it (it was built soon after, in 378 BC). As it was, they found the city unguarded and deserted, with most inhabitants having fled. They roamed about in wonder, breaking into the poorer houses, which had been locked – unlike the open doors of the homes of the elite.

The Gauls felt a sense of awe as they looked into those wealthy houses, where patricians awaited their fate, dressed in their full official regalia and seated in their courtyards – august, majestic, silent and calm, 'like statues in some holy place'. But then one of the Gauls touched the fashionably long beard of Marcus Papirius, who smashed his ivory staff down on the Gaul's head – and the butchery began.

Note the fact that the houses of the elite were open. Of course they were. In normal times they would be entertaining all manner of people and dealing with all manner of problems for most of the day – from *plebs* to the great and good: guests, clients, friends, business partners. But not on that day.

CAMILLUS TO THE RESCUE

It was inevitable that news of this assault would reach Camillus, to whom a message was relayed that the remaining senators had made him dictator: he should take whatever action was needed. He immediately called on Rome's allies to come to the rescue of the besieged city, and commandeered the troops who had taken refuge in Veii. He made a number of surprise attacks on the Gallic forces in the area, who were suffering from hunger as well as disease – situated as they were on the low, unhealthy, malaria-ridden grounds between the ridges of Rome.

SAVED BY THE GEESE

At one stage of the siege of Rome, the Gauls discovered a rocky path that led up to the top of the Citadel. After one of their men had checked out the route, they made the ascent. The terrain being what it was, it was not easy, and their weapons had to be passed from hand to hand as they pushed and pulled each other up the cliff, but they were not heard by the Roman guard or even the guard dogs. The Romans were saved by Juno's sacred geese, used for taking auspices, whose honking and clapping wings aroused the guard Marcus Manlius. He used his shield to knock backwards the one Gaul who had made his way up. As the man fell back down, he took a number of other Gauls with him. The rest of the Roman guard then woke up, and soon every Gaul had been sent tumbling down to the bottom of the cliff.

Eventually an armistice was agreed, with those besieged in the Citadel in Rome also at the end of their tether. The Gauls were bought off at the price of 1,000 pounds of gold. The Roman commander noted that the Gallic weights were heavier than the standard ones and remonstrated with Brennus, who threw his sword onto the scale with the words 'Vae victis' ('Anguish for the vanquished!').

This procedure, however, was interrupted by the unexpected arrival of Camillus. He ordered the gold to be taken back and told the Gauls to leave, denying that any agreement had been made. Battle in the ruins of the city at once broke out, and the Gauls were driven out – their camp taken and army annihilated.

REWARDS AND PUNISHMENT

The guard who had failed to spot the Gauls climbing up the Citadel was punished by being thrown off the Tarpeian Rock (p. 24). Every year from then on, in commemoration of the event, Juno's sacred geese were carried around in litters on gold and purple cushions – a way of honouring Juno as well as the geese – while guard dogs were executed on the Capitoline, as a warning always to stay on the alert.

WHAT NEXT FOR ROME?

Rome had been saved by the skin of its teeth, but what next? Since Rome was in ruins, and there had been much talk of some Romans moving to the magnificent city of Veii, just ten miles away, some of the tribunes argued that this would be the sensible option for the whole city. It took a passionate speech by Camillus, surrounded by the Senate, to dissuade them from that option.

He reminded the people of Rome's long history, especially its gods who had made their home there and the temples and sacred rituals established in their honour. He praised its location – its place in the middle of Italy, its ridges, the river connecting the city to the sea, the sea itself and the trading opportunities it provided for them (though it was not so near Rome as to present a threat from foreign fleets) – as well as its age, and Rome's success in defending itself against local enemies; and then there were all the indications from earliest times that Rome would be the seat of empire and master of the world.

Not everyone was persuaded by his words. But after Camillus had finished, as the Senate began debating another issue, soldiers returning from guard duty and passing through the Forum were ordered to halt, and the centurion said, 'We may as well stop here.' The Senate heard these words and took them as an omen, of which the milling crowd expressed its approval.

REBUILDING ROME

Livy tells us that the reconstruction of the city was not well planned. The state provided the tiles for roofing, and everyone was invited to cut timber and quarry stone for the buildings, which had to be completed within a year. It was all done in a great hurry and buildings were put up anywhere and everywhere, with property rights simply ignored.

The result was that the ancient sewers, which had originally been designed in a straight line following the original streets, now ran under people's houses, and the whole place looked like a squatters' settlement, not a properly planned city.

It would take Nero's rebuilding of Rome after the great fire of AD 64 – some 450 years later! – to get that particular area of Rome shipshape.

A SUMMARIZING INTERLUDE

The *plebs* had to a degree been successful in being granted land on which to settle and farm. They had also gone some way to ensuring a political say in the running of the Roman state.

But the one problem that had not been solved was that of debt. So, it is easy to understand that the seizure of the wealthy city of Veii, for example – which controlled some 200 square miles of territory, of which Rome probably took up to 140 square miles – encouraged the *plebs* even more in their determination to get their fair share.

There was no let-up in the fighting in the region. The Gallic sack of Rome egged on Rome's traditional rivals to take advantage of what they saw as a weakening of Rome's strength. Camillus was up to the task of reorganizing the Roman army and he soon dealt with attacks by the Volsci and Aequi – before turning his attention to Sutrium, an ally of Rome, which was under siege by the Etruscans. A huge number of captives were taken, and raised very large sums on the slave market.

In the course of these various wars, a number of towns came over to Rome's side; their inhabitants were admitted to citizenship and land was allotted to them. Meanwhile the Romans who had earlier settled in Veii were summoned back to Rome because they were needed for the rebuilding of the city. Despite the grumbling about this, a date was fixed for their return, with the threat of the loss of their rights if they did not do so. The result was that the rebuilding of Rome went on at pace, the state helping with the costs, and within a year the city was fully habitable. At the same time, work started on public buildings.

The tribunes raised the question of distributing among the *plebs* the land taken from the Volsci, but everyone was so hard at work rebuilding Rome that they could not turn their minds to the problem, and, even if they had been able to, in the circumstances they would have had no means of filling it with livestock.

385–384 BC: MARCUS MANLIUS' ATTEMPTED COUP

Manlius was the heroic soldier who had started the rout of the Gauls when they made an assault on the Roman troops defending the Citadel. Deeply envious of Camillus, he became the first patrician to actively take up the plebeian cause and work in concert with the plebeian tribunes.

While he was, of course, well aware of the problems of the distribution of land, he was also alert to the problem of debt among the *plebs*. This had been compounded by the rebuilding of Rome, which had left the *plebs* in even greater debt than usual, on top of the threat of chains and imprisonment. Manlius' possibly revolutionary ideas and the threat of war against a much-enlarged Volsci army, supported by the Latins and Hernici, spelled trouble. The Senate therefore appointed Aulus Cornelius Cossus dictator to deal with both crises. He first dealt with the external threat, and the war against the Volsci was won.

EXPANDING THE ARMY

Livy wonders how it could have been possible for the Volsci, who had been beaten so regularly by the Romans, to have enlarged their army so effectively. Recruiting successive generations of young men in between the wars? Recruiting from different clans? Or from areas deserted by Livy's time, inhabited once by free Romans, including *plebs*, but now only by slaves? (In Livy's time, Rome was a city of about a million people, which had drained the countryside of inhabitants.) Of course, the answer might simply be that the numbers of enemy troops were vastly exaggerated.

But Manlius was provided with an excuse for raising the debt issue when a centurion, well known for his military service, was hauled off for debt. He and his supporters intervened, and he spoke about the arrogance of the senators, the ruthlessness of the money-lenders, the misfortune of the *plebs* and the centurion's plight.

Manlius paid off the centurion's debt in full and released him. The centurion showed his scars from a succession of wars, explaining how he had tried to restore his ruined home and that, though he had paid off his debt many times, the interest on the loan had overwhelmed him. He committed himself to supporting Manlius.

Manlius responded by putting his own farm in Veii up for auction, saying that he would use the proceeds to ensure that no one else suffered the fate of the centurion. To the anger of the *plebs*, he added that the patricians were secretly hoarding Gallic gold that should have been held in the public treasury. Manlius did not tell them where it was hidden, but said that he would tell them in good time.

The dictator was summoned, and before a tribunal of the Senate and people the dictator instructed Manlius to say where this gold was hidden. Manlius accused him and the senators of being perfectly able to pay off people's debts as he had done, but because he did not answer the question he was arrested and taken off to prison. The *plebs* held their silence, because the order had come from the dictator.

They kept up the pressure on Manlius' behalf, however, and the Senate freed him – but the issue did not go away. During the period of peace after the Volsci war, Manlius began to plot revolution with the plebeians. 'Do you not outnumber everyone else?' he asked them. 'When it comes to war you are vastly superior to foreigners, but when it comes to the Senate you seem incapable of defending your freedom. Bring dictators and consuls down to your level, so that the Roman people can raise their heads!' he urged. He ended by declaring himself a patron of the *plebs*.

The Senate argued that this was a bid for kingly power and committed him to trial. The *plebs* reluctantly agreed that the charge was justified and Manlius was found guilty and thrown from the Tarpeian Rock – something of an irony, as that was where he had defended the Citadel against the Gallic attack in 390 BC.

381 BC: DAILY LIFE IN TUSCULUM

The people of Tusculum had an alliance with Rome, but some of them were found to have joined the army of the Volsci in the attack on the city. The Senate voted for Camillus to lead a campaign against the Tusculans, but when the army entered their territory there was no evidence that the Tusculans were going to try to defend it. Those working in the fields continued working, the gates of the city remained open, and citizens came out in their togas to greet them. The Roman army was even supplied with provisions.

FULL EMPLOYMENT

The emperor Hadrian was impressed by the people of Alexandria in Egypt. He wrote in a letter: 'No one is idle. Some are glass-blowers, others paper-makers, all at least are linen-weavers or seem to belong to one craft or another; the lame have their occupations, the eunuchs have theirs, the blind have theirs, and not even those whose hands are crippled are idle.'

When Camillus entered the city, he found all the houses with their doors open, the shops un-shuttered with all their goods on display, craftsmen hard at work, schools ringing with children's voices, and women and children mixing in the crowds as they hurried along the streets, wherever their business took them, showing no signs of fear or surprise. There were no indications of preparation for war at all. This is a unique picture of a working town.

Camillus was impressed, and, when the Tusculans came to Rome to explain how some had joined the Volsci against Rome, they were granted peace for the time being and, soon after, full citizenship.

380–377 BC: DEBT AGAIN

The problem of debt was always linked to the inability of the *plebs* to possess their own land. There was plenty of it (it was called *ager publicus*, 'common land'), but the rich simply commandeered it. With so much fighting to be done, the Senate had to raise military levies, which the tribunes insisted were just a way of preventing discussion about land for *plebs* and the associated debt problem.

Likewise, the appointment of censors, whose job it was to record accurately every Roman's wealth every year, was always being put off. The tribunes argued that the Senate was doing this on purpose because they did not want people to know the actual size of the debt. That, they claimed, would *prove* that one part of the state was being ruined by the other part (the landowners and the money-lenders), while the *plebs* were constantly being subjected to military service against ruthless enemies.

Eventually the tribunes managed to enforce one concession: that while the state was engaged in war, no one should have to pay tax or pass judgement on a case of debt.

But apart from that, nothing could be done – especially during times of peace, when the tribunes had no way of forcing the Senate into action because there was nothing significant enough (such as a war) for them to strike about.

371–366 BC: A PLEBEIAN CONSUL

A final resolution was reached, Livy tells us, only when the *plebs* realized that the key to success lay in getting their supporters into the positions of power that were dominated by the Senate.

Two such men put themselves forward: Gaius Licinius Stolo and Lucius Sextius (the first plebeian consul). They were duly elected and proposed three bills:

- First, that the interest paid on a debt should be subtracted from the amount borrowed, and the outstanding amount paid off in three annual instalments of equal size.

- Second, that no one should be allowed to own more than 500 *iugera* (c. 350 acres).

- Finally, that the post of military tribune, which had been dominated by the patricians, should be abolished, and one of the two consuls should be a *pleb*. There was nothing strictly prohibiting this: had not *plebs* been appointed to other official positions?

That, they argued, would show once and for all that the kings had been done away with, and that the *plebs* were free, and 'would share in power, honour, military glory, standing and nobility – great things to enjoy, and still greater to leave to their children'.

These proposals were very controversial. But those supporting them pointed out that most *plebs* had a property that could barely sustain the necessities of life or even provide a burial place. Did anyone really need *more* than 500 *iugera*? That could be divided up among 300 poor citizens to live off!

Despite the controversy, the battle for land for the *plebs* was finally (in principle) won; the legislation was passed and celebrated with the Great Games. But now that a *pleb* could become a consul, would he still act in the interest of *plebs*?!

In 366 BC Camillus died and was called a 'second Romulus'.

A HYPOCRITICAL SENATOR

It was through the good offices of Stolo that the *plebs* were given the power to stand for the consulship. He had also passed a law that nobody should possess more than 300 acres of public land, but he himself bought 600 acres, so to cover up his crime he gave half the property to his son. He was prosecuted and became the first victim of his own law. Thus, he showed that nobody should give a command that they are not prepared to carry out themselves.

Valerius Maximus

364 BC: HOW MUSICAL SHOWS STARTED

Rome was struck by a dreadful plague in 354 BC, which did not yield to any of the usual ceremonies to get rid of it. The Romans therefore, says Livy, invented a new entertainment (up to that date, the only one had been chariot racing): dancing to the sound of the pipe without any singing of songs. Young Romans then started adding jokes and crude verses, with gestures to fit the words, and these were modified into dancing in time with musical medleys.

Some time later, a certain Livius Andronicus turned this into a one-man show complete with plot, backed up by a pipe player and a boy to sing the songs. When professionals took over this format, the young went back to the old system of playing it for laughs in verse. The art of Roman drama was gradually developed from this. Livy contrasts such humble beginnings with the situation at the time he was writing – when putting on plays cost a king's fortune!

Unfortunately, this ceremony/entertainment proved no more efficient at ending the plague than the others, though it was later remembered that the plague was finally alleviated when Lucius Manlius, 'the imperious', was nominated dictator and promptly hammered a nail into the wall of the temple of Jupiter Best and Greatest, naturally nailing the plague at once.

362 BC: MANLIUS AND HIS SON

Unfortunately, hammering in the nail was not enough for the bully Lucius Manlius. He was very keen to wage war against the Hernici, and in attempting to raise a levy for this he did not hesitate to fine the *plebs*, flog them or imprison them if they did not obey (and he was equally severe on his very own family). This did not make him popular, and he was brought to trial.

What particularly outraged the *plebs* was Manlius' treatment of his son, whom for no reason at all he banished from the city, his home and the Forum, consigning him to servile labour. The reason for this treatment was simply that the son had a speech defect and had problems expressing himself. Why, even dumb animals did not treat weak offspring like that!

All this was very distressing to his son, who did not like to think that he was responsible for his father's unpopularity. So, concealing a knife on his person, he managed to gain an audience with the tribune who had brought the charges against his father. The terrified tribune agreed to abandon the charges, and was quite open about why, but the *plebs* would have been only too happy to punish Manlius, come what may, such was the general admiration for the son's behaviour – a fine example of filial piety.

A PLEBEIAN CONSUL AS GENERAL

Lucius Genucius was the first plebeian consul to be put in charge of a war, in this case against the Hernici. Rome was on tenterhooks: would he, a *pleb*, be up to the job?

It was soon clear what the answer was: he marched out of the city straight into an ambush, in which he was killed, before his army took flight. The patricians were absolutely furious, and made their feelings about the situation very plain: the gods themselves had taken revenge and punished the Romans for allowing the auspices to be taken by a *pleb* and not, as the gods had long ago ordained, by a patrician. But the army was regrouped by Gaius Sulpicius and drove the Hernici back, and, though both sides reinforced themselves, the Romans were eventually victorious.

357 BC: AN ARMY MAKES THE LAW!

A proposal was made by the Senate that a 5 per cent tax should be levied on the price attendant on the freeing of a slave. It was agreed that this would go a long way to restoring Rome's finances. But this was put not to an assembly in Rome, but unofficially by the consul to the army camped outside Rome, voting in tribes. This was quite unprecedented, but the law was passed. The tribunes were relaxed about this happening because they were in favour of it, but insisted that it never happen again. They were afraid of what damage might be done if soldiers in camp outside Rome, who had sworn a military oath to the consul, were asked to pass a law *against* the *plebs'* interests.

The vote was a significant moment: the soldier-*plebs* were being given a *positive* sense of their political clout – beyond just refusing to sign up for the levy. Perhaps elite power was trembling a little more on its throne?

356 BC: A PLEBEIAN DICTATOR

The patricians were appalled when the plebeian Gaius Rutulus was appointed dictator against a dangerous alliance of enemies, and he appointed another plebeian to be his deputy. They tried everything they could to prevent this happening, but their disapproval simply made the *plebs* more eager that it should.

In the event, Gaius took 8,000 prisoners and cleared the enemy out of Roman territory and was given a triumph by the *plebs*, though without the Senate's authorization.

352 BC: THE DEBT PROBLEM SOLVED?

While the tribunes continued to oppose senatorial efforts to ensure that the consuls were not plebeian, the *plebs* were much more concerned that the increasing interest they had to pay on debt could not be sustained, and public disturbances became common. The Senate finally gave in and a plebeian consul was appointed to sort the problem out.

A board of five 'bankers' was appointed by the consuls to deal with it. They either had the treasury pay the debt off, having first secured a guarantee that the debtor would eventually cough up, or they examined the debtor's property (on which the loan would have been taken) and decided what a fair price for it was. In this way vast debts were wiped, without complaints from the parties on either side.

350 BC: A SIGNIFICANT UTTERANCE

News then came of a huge Gallic army advancing into Latium. Having defeated one half of the army, the exhausted Romans found themselves up against the other half and, in rousing the troops to action, the consul Marcus Popilius Laenas cried, 'What are you holding back for, men? These are not Latins or Sabines that you're fighting, men you can turn into allies once you have defeated them, but wild animals. We must shed their blood or give them ours!'

THE ROMAN SECRET OF SUCCESS

Four hundred years later, the emperor Claudius would say almost exactly the same thing when explaining what it was that had given Rome its empire: it was Rome's extraordinary ability to turn enemies into friends. In learning how to do that while they conquered Italy, the Romans had acquired the skills required to repeat the trick when they were defeating enemies abroad.

Incidentally, Livy comments that the eventual victory over the Gauls was especially sweet for the *plebs*, because the consul who had led the army – Popilius – was a plebeian. Did the patricians, the *plebs* mused, still regret that a *pleb* could be consul?

PLEB POWER: A SUMMARY OF GAINS

378 BC: It was decided that, while the state was engaged in war, no one should have to pay tax or pass judgement on a case of debt.

371 BC: The debt problem was mostly alleviated; it was decreed that no one should be allowed to own more than 500 *iugera* (c. 350 acres) of land; the post of military tribune, which had been dominated by the patricians, was abolished and it was decided that one of the two consuls should be a *pleb* (the first was Lucius Sextius).

356 BC: Gaius Rutulus became the first plebeian dictator.

VII

THE CONQUEST
OF ITALY AND
THE TRIUMPH OF
THE PLEBS:

350–280 BC

This chapter reworks the usual temporal arrangement of the story by dealing very briefly with the important consequences of the battle against the Latin League, and the extensive and very brutal war against the Samnites, both of which finally established Rome as the master of most of Italy.

It then wraps up in short order a number of other important developments (out of strict temporal sequence) that finally left the *plebs* on an equal political footing with the patricians, and ends by briefly summarizing the stages by which that *plebs* vs. patricians 'conflict of the orders', arising from the establishment of the republic in 509 BC, had been finally resolved.

341–338 BC: THE LATIN LEAGUE:
TURNING ENEMIES INTO FRIENDS

Rome had been fighting its neighbours for hundreds of years, as we have seen, but now came a turning point that would eventually bring all the Latin towns that had formed themselves into a league into alliance with Rome. The most important feature of this new alliance was that *every member of it supplied manpower for the Roman army and could expect Roman protection if attacked.*

There were four different categories of relationship:

- Self-ruling citizen colonies planted by Rome across Italy.

- Independent communities with various ties to Rome.

- Communities in a defensive alliance with Rome.

- Communities with full Roman citizenship, with or without the right to vote.

Communities could also change their status if Rome felt they deserved it.

This flexible system of incorporations and alliances was Rome's way of turning enemies into friends and largely keeping them friends. Further, it was the key to ensuring Rome's armies were up to strength, a critical factor in the forthcoming fight to the death against the Carthaginian invaders under Hannibal (218–202 BC).

The system obviously gave Italian citizens a political status and focus of loyalty beyond their own community, which over time would turn millions into citizens of the Roman Empire. This was especially true of the *plebs* who did the actual fighting and would be responsible for the growth and security of the empire.

340 BC: THE HEROISM OF DECIUS MUS

The battle against the Latins was not going well and the consul Publius Decius Mus asked Marcus Valerius, the state pontiff of Rome, to 'dictate the formula whereby I may devote myself to save the legions'. He then leapt onto his horse and 'fully armed rode into the midst of the enemy – a sight to admire for both armies, almost superhuman in its nobility, as if sent from heaven to expiate all anger of the gods and deflect disaster from his own people to the Latins'. The result was that 'wherever he rode, men shrank away as though struck by some death-dealing star', and when he finally fell beneath a rain of missiles, there was no doubt that the Latins were in complete confusion, and they scattered and fled.

Livy then discusses what happened after a man so sacrificed himself, and writes: 'these details I have thought it appropriate to repeat, in the very words in which they were formulated and handed down, although the memory of every practice, religious and secular, has been effaced by our preference for all that is new and foreign in place of what is native and traditional'.

343–341 BC: THE FIRST SAMNITE WAR

The years of conflict against the Latins were followed by an even harder struggle against the Samnites and their allies (including Latins). Involving long and difficult battles against a particularly ferocious and relentless enemy, this war would prove to be vital experience for what was to come.

The Samnites were a tribe that did not dwell in towns or cities but on hilltops, and they had such a reputation for violence that the Greeks thought their name derived from the word for 'spear'. Every Samnite male grave contained weapons, most of which were indeed spears. The Romans called them 'pitiless'; the geographer Strabo described them as 'animals'.

342 BC: MILITARY DISAFFECTION

The first contact with the Samnites ended in a Roman victory in 341 BC. But some of the Roman soldiers sent to protect the Campanians from Samnite attack wondered why *they* should enjoy the luxuries of Capua, when it was the Roman *plebs* who had done all the fighting but were still farming poor land around Rome and paying off interest on debts. They hatched a plot to take the city themselves, but it was discovered and an army was sent out to deal with them. In the event, it was agreed that the disaffected soldiers had a case and would not be punished for their treachery.

340 BC: 'THE COMMANDS OF MANLIUS'

On account of a divine warning, the Roman consul Manlius gave strict instructions to the army not to take to the field against the army they were currently facing, made up of Samnite and Latin soldiers, until so ordered. But the consul's son Titus Manlius, riding close to the enemy's position, was recognized by the enemy commander, Geminus Maecius, who challenged Titus to a duel.

Unable to resist the challenge, 'or through the invincible power of destiny', Titus took Maecius on and killed him. After gathering up the spoils, he rode back to the camp, the cheers of the army ringing in his ears. His father immediately summoned an assembly and began:

> Titus Manlius, you have respected neither consular authority
> nor your father's dignity; you have left your position to
> fight the enemy in defiance of my order... As far as my own
> feelings are concerned, they are stirred by a man's natural love
> for his children, as well as by the example you have given of
> your courage, even though this was marred by a false concep-
> tion of glory... But since consular authority must either be
> confirmed by your death or annulled for ever by your going
> unpunished, I believe that you yourself, if you have any drop
> of my blood in you, would agree that the military discipline
> which you undermined by your error must be restored by
> your punishment. Go, lictor, bind him to the stake.

The young man was executed and buried with full military honours. The 'Commands of Manlius', a stern lesson in discipline and grim warning for the future, had the desired effect.

321–304 BC: THE SECOND SAMNITE WAR

321 BC: Though not an actual defeat for Rome, since no battle was fought, the Roman army found itself trapped by the Samnites in a mountainous area known as the Caudine Forks and had no

option but to surrender. The whole army was humiliated by being forced to walk 'under a yoke' of surrender but otherwise, for what appear to be political reasons, they were just stripped of their armour and allowed to walk free.

314 BC: The people of Sora had decided to go over to the side of the Samnites and, having slaughtered all their Roman colonists, welcomed them in. The Romans wanted revenge on the Samnites, and their army duly took it, but even more than that they wanted to avenge the slaughter of the colonists.

Sora was not the easiest place to attack, but a traitor from the town showed them how it could be done. And it was. The 225 who were identified as leading the revolt against Rome and organizing the massacre of the colonists were brought to Rome and flogged and beheaded in the Forum.

Livy comments on the joy this brought to the *plebs*, 'who felt strongly about guaranteeing the security of their own people wherever they were sent out as colonists' – an example of *pleb* solidarity with those who had wanted to improve their life by moving to pastures new. Many extended families would have taken advantage of such offers, especially if they had only small holdings in Rome and wanted to ensure their family's future. After all, such holdings divided up between sons over a generation or so became so small as to be valueless.

298–290 BC: THE THIRD SAMNITE WAR

296 BC: An effort was made to protect an area the Samnites had just raided by sending Roman colonists there. But it turned out

to be very difficult to find *plebs* who would agree to go, since they believed they were being sent not to settle the land but simply to provide a perpetual outpost in a hostile area. Given the *plebs'* long experience of what it was like to possess farmland that was likely to be attacked by enemies at any time – and so suffer the loss of all their property, cattle and crops – their response was not surprising.

A DISGRACED CENTURION

During that war the centurion Marcus Laetorius was summoned before the *plebs* because he had attempted to seduce one of his subordinates. He went into exile and committed suicide for shame. But even so he was found guilty on a charge of sexual immorality by the verdict of the entire *plebs*. The army standards, the consecrated eagles, and that most reliable guardian of the Roman Empire, our strict military discipline, followed him all the way into the underworld.

Valerius Maximus

295 BC: The battle of Sentinum saw the Romans facing a formidable alliance of Samnites, Etruscans, Umbrians and Gauls. There was still a lingering sense that patrician generals were better than plebeian ones, but the patrician Quintus Fabius and the *pleb* Publius Decius (son of his father, p. 141) had worked together for a long time and the Romans were delighted when they both set off to

take command of operations. Rome's victory broke up the defeated coalition, and the Etruscans, Umbrians and Senone Gauls pulled out of the war. The Samnites, besides losing their allies, suffered heavy casualties.

The Romans went on to win other battles against the Samnites. In the final stage of the war, which ended five years later, the Romans devastated Samnium and the Samnites capitulated.

THE PROPER USE OF WOOD

Marching towards the enemy, Quintus Fabius found some men protected by an armed guard collecting wood. 'What for?' he demanded. 'Firewood,' they said. 'But have you not got ramparts?' replied Fabius. 'Yes,' came the reply, 'double ramparts and a ditch.' 'That's quite enough wood,' said Fabius. 'Use that.' And they did.

Fabius' point was that an army had no business being settled in one place. It needed to be mobile and physically fit for action.

290 BC: The Samnite wars finally ended. By that time, Rome had drawn most of Italy within its control, creating fourteen new colonies.

A GREAT OLD ROMAN

The consul Manius Curius Dentatus (Dentatus because, we are told, he was born with teeth) was an important figure in the fight against the ferocious Samnite hill clans. In 290 BC, he was approached by some Samnites with a massive bribe of gold. They found him seated on a crude bench by his hearth in his farmhouse, roasting turnips, eating from a rough wooden dish. Slightly amazed, they invited him to take the bribe, but he laughed in their faces, calling them 'ambassadors on a superfluous, not to say incompetent, mission'. He told them to take back their gift, 'as noxious as it was costly', and to bear in mind that he could 'neither be beaten in battle nor corrupted by money bribes'. Further, that 'there was no glory in possessing wealth, but only in controlling its possessors'.

When he had thrashed the Samnites and celebrated a triumph, the people wanted to give Dentatus a vast chunk of land as a reward. But he refused and settled for the handout that the Senate had decreed for the *plebs*, reckoning that 'no one could be counted a suitable citizen of the republic who could not be satisfied with what everybody else was given'.

So much – very briefly – for the savage wars against the Samnites.

342–300 BC: FURTHER CONCESSIONS TO THE PLEBS

We now return – out of chronological sequence – to a series of inter-vening events in Rome important to the struggle between *plebs* and patricians. Since the background to these incidents has already been covered, only the new developments are detailed. Among them are a string of important concessions. One senses that the plebeian struggle was coming to a climax.

342 BC: Back in Rome, it was proposed that:

1. Lending money on interest should be forbidden;

2. No one should hold any office twice within ten years;

3. It was permissible for both consuls to be plebeians.

These were considerable concessions, as Livy writes, but he had his doubts whether they were in fact actually granted because they were recorded only by certain authors.

339 BC: Three laws were proposed that were 'greatly in favour of the *plebs* and unfavourable to the Senate':

1. The decrees of the *plebs* should apply to every Roman citizen (this may only have been proposed, but not enacted).

2. At least one of the censors should be a plebeian.

3. The Senate no longer had the right to withhold approval from a law enacted by the *plebs*, though they could still try.

340 bc: A rebel army of Latins and Campanians was defeated by the Romans. The captured land was divided up among the

plebs, each receiving up to three *iugera*, with extra for those moving further away from Rome.

326 BC: As Livy proudly announces in his history, 'this year the liberty of the Roman people had a second birth with the abolition of enslavement for debt'.

A handsome young boy, Publilius, had put himself in the power of the moneylender Lucius Papirius, because his father owed Lucius money. Lucius attempted to seduce him, failed, and ordered him to be stripped and lashed. The boy ran into the street, protesting against Lucius' lechery and ruthlessness.

There was an outcry. The Senate was convened and ruled that imprisonment for debt was banned and only a debtor's possessions, not his person, could be seized.

318 BC: The Plebeian Assembly legislated that the membership of the Senate should be determined not, as before, by the consuls or other officials but by the censors.

311 BC: Up to now, the right to command a fighting unit had been almost exclusively in the gift of consuls and dictators. But in another concession, the *plebs* won the right to elect sixteen military tribunes to serve in four legions and two naval commissioners to be in charge of equipping and refitting the fleet.

299 BC: An earlier law decreed that no official could execute a citizen without him being allowed to appeal. If he lost, a new law called it a 'wicked act' to flog or behead him. Livy commented that in those modest days, that was condemnation enough; in his day, it would have been laughed at.

330–287 BC: FURTHER EVENTS AND THE FINAL BREAKTHROUGH

330 BC: The Volsci town of Privernum launched an attack on Rome – but, as ever, was brought into alliance. As the Priverni said, if they had a good peace, it would be kept loyally and be permanent; if a bad one, it would not last long. The Romans saw this as the mark of a people that wanted liberty, and as such were worthy of becoming Romans.

At the same time news came of an uprising of Gauls. The leader chosen to take on the Gauls was told to enlist an army without making any exceptions. The result was that even tradesmen and sedentary labourers – 'types quite unsuitable for military service' – were drafted. But it turned out to be a false alarm.

DRUNKEN PIPERS

There had to be pipers playing at every sacrifice, but in 311 BC, annoyed at not being allowed to hold their feast in the temple of Jupiter, the pipers went on strike and walked off to Tibur (Tivoli), nearly twenty miles away, leaving no one to play. The Senate approached the Tiburtines and asked them to find a way of sending them back. Trying to persuade the pipers proved pointless, so the Tiburtines came up with a cunning trick. During a public holiday, the citizens invited the pipers into their houses to play while they were eating and, since they knew the pipers liked their drink, got them all completely plastered. Then they dumped them, sound asleep, into carts and had them dragged back to Rome and left in the Forum. The *plebs* persuaded the pipers to stay, and they were given permission on three days a year to roam around the streets in fancy dress, piping away for fun, as they still did, with their rights to a feast in the temple restored.

310 BC: Another Appius Claudius (his great-great-grandfather was the hated decemvir, p. 94) stayed true to his family name when, having been censor for the allotted period of eighteen months, he decided to hang on to power. When it came to the vote, although three plebeian tribunes voted against him, three voted for him. To everyone's disgust he remained in office. Here was another example of plebeian tribunes of sufficient wealth and influence who were sympathetic to the patrician class.

While the struggle for political power between patricians and plebeians was becoming less acute, it was still the case that any Roman who had been a slave and was subsequently freed (becoming a freedman) could be the subject of some discrimination (p. 214).

One such was the plebeian Gnaeus Flavius, the first freedman to hold the office of aedile (in charge of Rome's streets, markets, temples, water supply and games). In that role, he ensured that important legal knowledge was made accessible to everyone, by publishing accounts of legal proceedings and the days on which public business could be done (he wrote up those days on whiteboards all around the Forum for everyone to see). The senators usually kept that knowledge to themselves.

On one occasion he was visiting a sick friend, and the young nobles sitting around his bed refused to rise when Flavius came in. He ordered his official chair to be brought, from which he looked down upon his furious enemies. The tide was turning against the nobles, as other developments would illustrate.

304 BC: Lower tradesmen and craftsmen were granted membership of the Plebeian Assembly and the power to vote. This had previously been denied them because they were not deemed capable of becoming soldiers (p. 46). Sons of freedmen were also admitted. Slavery was ubiquitous in the ancient world, of course, but the Romans seem to be the only people to have given all *freed* slaves a form of citizenship that turned into full citizenship for their sons and their family for the rest of time.

300 BC: Livy comments that Rome's main enemies, the Etruscans and the Samnites, were still abiding by their truces, while Rome's successes had given them much land on which they could establish plebeian colonies. But peace at home and abroad did not stop tribunes making trouble – in this instance by proposing a law that priesthoods and the right to take auguries, up until then confined to patricians, should be opened to those plebeians who, having won consulships and triumphs, deserved the full hand of official privileges.

But though the patricians maintained the argument that the resulting rituals would be defiled, Livy reports that: 'The patricians were now accustomed to being the losers in conflicts like that. Once used to seeing their political enemies not bothering to aim for the top offices because they were completely out of reach for them, against all their expectations they now saw the *plebs* holding those positions themselves – consulships, censorships, and triumphs.'

It came to a crunch in a 'violent confrontation' between Appius Claudius (who else?) and the plebeian consul Publius Decius Mus, who pointed out that his plebeian father had once ritually sacrificed himself to save the army from defeat, which did not suggest the gods had been angry with him (p. 141). And if war broke out, he said, the Senate and the Roman people could pin their hopes as securely on plebeian generals as they had done on patrician ones.

> What is wrong for such men to take on the insignia of priests and augurs? They have been honoured with special chairs, the purple-edged toga, the palm-embroidered tunic, the triumphal crown and laurel wreaths. Their homes have been marked out by having the enemy's spoils attached to them. Should the man who, dressed in the robes of Jupiter Best and Greatest, has ridden through the city in a golden chariot to ascend to the Capitol *not* be seen with the sacrificial cup and the curved staff when, with his head covered, he slaughters the sacrificial animal, to take the auguries? If in the inscription below a man's portrait, the words 'consulship, censorship, triumph' can be read with equanimity, so surely can be the words 'augur, pontiff'?

The law 'with great acclamation' was passed, adding a further feather to the cap of the plebeians in their battle for political equality.

297 BC: Another tussle for the consulship between patrician and *pleb*. The notorious Appius Claudius, desperate that he should not be joined by a *pleb* as consul, used all his influence to try to make Quintus Fabius his co-consul. Fabius refused, despite the plea of other nobles (i.e. other ex-consuls) 'to lift the consulship out of the plebeian mire and restore both to the office and to the patrician families the dignity of former times'. As a result, a plebeian was elected.

295 BC: THE SHRINE OF PLEBEIAN CHASTITY

Verginia was a patrician married to a *pleb* and, because she had married outside her rank, was prevented from playing her part in the various ceremonies associated with that patrician shrine. But Verginia insisted she was chaste and that she had been given to her husband as an unmarried girl and was proud of him and everything he had achieved. She set up an altar in her house to 'plebeian chastity', to which she invited married, chaste plebeian women to tend it as reverently and purely as the other shrine. Unfortunately, it was visited by unchaste women from all different walks of life, and was eventually abandoned.

THE MELLOWING OF THE PLEB–PATRICIAN CONFLICT

294 BC: We have already encountered moments when tribunes of the *plebs* supported the Senate. This is another. The consul Postumius had won a signal victory in Etruria, allied with the Samnites, and wanted to celebrate a triumph, but his personal enemies were against it. The plebeian tribunes were split on the issue: he was supported by three but opposed by seven plus the whole Senate. The issue was then successfully raised before the Plebeian Assembly, and Postumius said he would have raised it himself but was sure he would be blocked by tribunes 'sucking up to the nobility'. But the support of the Plebeian Assembly was all he needed, and the *plebs* made it a day of celebration.

THE ROMAN TRIUMPH

Anyone who won a triumph was urged to remember he was mortal. Song and dance accompanied pictures of captured cities, displays of bullion and coin, and enemy generals in chains, all culminating in the *triumphator* himself, with his army, wearing a crown of gold and precious stones and dressed in a purple toga inwoven with gold stars – a god for a day. Behind him stood a public slave, whispering in his ear throughout the ceremony, 'Remember you are mortal.' His army backed up the message with mocking and often filthy chants about him. When Julius Caesar celebrated a triumph for his conquest of Gaul, the soldiers sang, 'Romans, watch out for your wives – the bald adulterer's home. / Fucked his way in Gaul through a fortune, borrowed here in Rome.'

That incident reinforces the point that there were always plebeians – presumably rich ones – who leaned towards the Senate in certain situations. At the same time, because there was now little serious distinction politically between patrician and *pleb*, the old battle lines were no longer as divisive as they once were. The political always has social consequences.

But Papirius was not so popular in 293 BC when he won a thumping victory against the Samnites, bringing with him 2,533,000 pounds of bronze from the sale of captives and 1,830 pounds of silver, all of which was handed to the treasury and none to the soldiers. This caused great resentment among the *plebs* because tax was being demanded from them to pay the troops. Livy suggests that Papirius wanted the glory of pouring foreign wealth into the state coffers. After all, he was a patrician and presumably felt the Senate was the best judge of how the money should be spent.

287 BC: THE FINAL POLITICAL BREAKTHROUGH

The secession by the *plebs* in 494 BC resulted in the first effort to try to solve the problem of debt among the poor (p. 71). As we have seen, that took the form of measures to give the *plebs* a degree of political power over the patrician Senate. But despite a raft of measures to get a grip on the question (pp. 71, 131, 136), it was not resolved, and in 287 BC there was another major walkout of the *plebs*, this time over the River Tiber on to the Janiculum. A dictator, Quintus Hortensius, was appointed to deal with it, and he decided that only a radical political decision would finally close the case, which one of our historical sources records as follows:

> The patricians said that plebiscites [laws produced by votes of the *plebs*] did not apply to them because they had been passed without their authority, but later on Hortensius passed a law which decreed that plebiscites applied to *everyone*.

In other words, full political parity between *pleb* and patrician was now restored. Senatorial authority was no longer required to ratify any decision taken by the Plebeian Assembly *and that Assembly now became Rome's most important legislative body*. Since it was the wealthy who did the lending, the *plebs* were now in a position to find ways of creating a fairer system.

It was certainly not before time. Rome's successful battles with the Samnites had confirmed them as the most powerful state in Italy. Further conflicts over the military levy and debt did no one any favours. Likewise, integrating wealthy plebeians into the elite was an intelligent way of co-opting plebeian power across the board and perhaps made the old noble engage more creatively with this new world, without affecting the oligarchic nature of Roman rule. It certainly gave the Roman people as a whole more of an active sense about what it meant to be Roman.

But the big question was: how would this realignment of power be used *in practice*?

FROM TYRANNY TO FREEDOM:
A SUMMARY

509 BC: Rome's last tyrant king was thrown out, and the elites who had advised him at once took over the new republic as senators and annually appointed leaders (officials such as consuls, etc.). And the *plebs*? Desperate for change, they found none: poverty, debt and landlessness persisted. They took action by rioting and withdrawing their labour, especially on the battlefield (pp. 81–2).

507 BC: The *plebs* won the right to appeal against arrest.

494 BC: The Senate agree to the election of two 'tribunes of the *plebs*.' Their person was sacrosanct, they could monitor the Senate's proceedings, intervene against an official's ruling and veto any senatorial laws.

471 BC: The tribunes, upped in number to five, were to be appointed by a Plebeian Assembly, so that patricians had no say.

457 BC: The number of plebeian tribunes was increased to ten.

451–450 BC: Rome had no official law codes, and the laws that existed were under the strict control of the Senate. The first *public* code of law – the Ten (which soon became the Twelve) Tables – removed arbitrary legal decision-making.

449 BC: For the first time, the *plebs* demanded a triumph

be celebrated, without Senate agreement.

448 BC: Patricians were co-opted as plebeian tribunes.

445 BC: Mixed patrician–*pleb* marriage was permitted.
The consuls were replaced with military tribunes
with consular authority, to be appointed from
both patricians and *plebs*.

406 BC: Soldiers were to be paid out of public funds.

367 BC: There was some mitigation of the debt problem.
It was decreed that no one should be allowed
to own more than 500 *iugera* (c. 350 acres) of
land. One of the two consuls *had* to be a plebeian
(eventually both could be – this first happened
much later, in 172 BC).

356 BC: The first plebian dictator.

342 BC: Lending money on interest was forbidden. It
was also ruled that no one should hold any office
twice within ten years.

326 BC: Enslavement for debt was abolished. A debtor's
property could be seized, but not his person.

318 BC: The power to appoint senators was removed
from the Senate and placed in the hands of the
censors.

311 BC: The *plebs* gained the right to appoint
commanders to a fighting unit.

304 BC: Gnaeus Flavius, son of an ex-slave (see p. 151),
used his authority as an official to publish
'details of civil law kept in secret religious

archives' and 'dates when legal cases could be brought', all closely guarded by the senators but of vital importance for any *pleb* wishing to go to law. Lower tradesmen and craftsmen, and freed slaves, were granted membership of the Plebeian Assembly and the power to vote.

300 BC: The major priesthoods were opened to the *plebs*. Plebeian consuls were allowed to take the auguries.

299 BC: Further protection for *plebs* appealing their cases.

287 BC: Plebeian laws became binding for the whole people, and the battle was over: the balance between Senatorial authority and the freedom of the *plebs* was secured. All the decrees of the Senate were to be made publicly available in the temple of Ceres.

VIII

THE BEGINNING
OF EMPIRE:

280–167 BC

So far the Roman *plebs* had been fighting their battles against Italians and occasionally Gauls on *home* soil. That would change dramatically over the next 150 years as Rome dealt with the Spartan warrior Pyrrhus and turned its thoughts to Carthage in North Africa and to the wider Greek world.

It is not surprising that the Latin for 'at home and abroad' was *domi militiaeque* (meaning 'at home [compare English 'domicile'] and on military campaign').

280–275 BC: PYRRHIC VICTORIES

Greeks had been living in southern Italy since the eighth century BC, and so many migrated there that it was referred to as 'Enlarged Greece' (*Magna Graecia*). Its 'capital' was Tarentum – founded in 725 BC mostly by Spartans, who engaged in constant battles with local peoples. But they were now feeling increasingly threatened by the speed with which Rome was gaining control over Italy. So they invited Pyrrhus, a famous and very imaginative Spartan general, to come to their aid.

THE NAME OF ITALY

The Romans thought that the Greeks who had settled in southern Italy were so impressed by its extraordinary fertility that they drew on the early Latin word *viteliu* (young bull) to call that part of Italy (V)*Italia*. Slowly the name caught on for the whole of the country, which by the time of Augustus extended as far as the Alps.

Pyrrhus' army arrived complete with elephants. These terrified the Romans, but they discovered that elephants were terrified of horses, which they trained to drive them off.

Pyrrhus won both the battles he fought against Rome, but the price was so high that he ruefully commented, 'If we win one more battle against the Romans, it will be the end of us,' and withdrew. Hence 'Pyrrhic victory'.

THE SIZE OF THE ROMAN STATE

By now Rome had grown from a state of about 775 square miles in 340 BC to 5,900 square miles in 280 BC (almost the size of Yorkshire)! The census of 265 BC numbers adult male Roman citizens at 292,234, and the Greek diplomat Polybius (p. 179) puts total Roman manpower across Italy at 730,000.

264–241 BC: ROME'S FIRST WAR AGAINST CARTHAGE

Carthage was a colony of the Phoenicians, who lived on a coastal strip stretching from Syria to Lebanon and Galilee. We do not know what they actually called themselves because they refer to themselves only as inhabitants of various cities ('inhabitants of Tyre/Sidon/Byblos', and so on). The Bible lumps them all together as Canaanites or Philistines.

THE SOURCE OF OUR ALPHABET

To simplify: in the eighth century BC, the ancient Greeks took the twenty-two symbols that made up the Phoenician consonantal alphabet and adapted them to make the Greek alphabet, adding vowels. So Phoenician *aleph* became Greek *alpha* A/α (our A/a), *beth* became Greek *beta* B/β (our B/b), *gimel* became Greek *gamma* Γ/γ (our G/g), and so on. These were adapted by the Etruscans and the Romans adapted those, turning them into the Roman alphabet (*alpha bet-a*) – which they spread all over their empire and which eventually became the European alphabet we use today. Both Greek and Roman literature was composed in capital letters with NOGAPSBETWEENTHEWORDS. The earliest example of English is the law code of King Æthelberht of Kent (reigned c. AD 589–616) though it survives only in a later manuscript. The oldest poem is *Caedmon's Hymn*, c. 650.

The importance of the Phoenician alphabet lay in the fact that it was *simple*. Anyone could learn how to use it. Writing was no longer the preserve of the political and religious elites.

The Greeks called them *Phoinikes*, which they pronounced 'poi-nik-ess'. The Romans latinized that name to *Punici* (our 'Punic') and *Poeni*. *Phoinos* means 'red' and the name perhaps referred to the copper colour of their skin and/or their expertise in the purple dye industry.

PURPLE DYE

The Phoenicians were famous for their dye, Tyrian (after the city of Tyre) purple – the colour worn by Roman senators, emperors and later royalty. It was made from the mucus of the murex shellfish, whose glands were extracted, placed in lead containers and heated with brine for ten days. This dye could then be modified to produce various shades of colour.

The date-palm is also called *Phoenix,* and so is the bird – both, it was believed, originated from that area.

The Phoenicians were the Mediterranean's greatest traders and founded Carthage (modern Tunis) in the ninth century BC. By 700 BC Carthage had moved into Sardinia, founded several colonies in Sicily – including Palermo, with its fine natural harbour – and established communities in Malaga, Marbella and Alicante. Carthaginians were to become dominant figures along the North African coast, and in southern Spain, western Sicily and Sardinia.

Interestingly, Carthage had long been aware that Rome was a rising, and possibly rival, power. It had already made a treaty with Rome in 507 BC, which was ratified a number of times over the centuries (p. 64).

THE FIRST PUNIC WAR: 264–241 BC

At a time when Carthage was master of most of Sicily, Rome seized Messina, about three miles across the straits from the toe of Italy. Rome's reasoning may have been that, Sicily being a stone's throw from Italy, Carthage might be tempted to invade in the way that Pyrrhus had done. Better therefore to stop them in their tracks before they even began.

While the Romans were pretty much masters of land battles, the First Punic War would have to be won at sea against the greatest seafaring nation in the Mediterranean – a very different kettle of fish. The challenge to Rome was to build a fleet capable of taking on the Carthaginians.

BUILDING A FLEET

When their original fleet was destroyed in a storm, the Romans rebuilt the whole fleet in the extraordinary time of three months. How? With skilled *pleb* artisans, who learned fast, thanks to a lucky strike. We are told that, after one encounter, a Carthaginian warship ran aground and fell into Roman hands. They promptly constructed a fleet on that model. While that building was going on, the *plebs* were practising their new rowing skills – on land.

But winning a battle at sea was another matter, given Rome's complete lack of experience. The Romans therefore decided to turn a sea battle into a land battle.

On the bow of each ship, *pleb* artisans attached a massive metal ram and on deck a *corvus* (literally 'crow') – a gangplank with a huge spike at the far end. Instead of all the subtle manoeuvring for position required in a sea battle between oared ships, at which the Carthaginians were expert, the Roman plan was simplicity itself. Load each ship with as many Roman soldiers as possible, row at speed straight into the side of the enemy ship, slam down the *corvus* into its deck, locking the two ships together, and send in the army to slaughter the crew.

The Romans won, and from 241 BC took control of Sicily, and in 238 BC Corsica and Sardinia, soon to become the first Roman provinces, ready to be exploited in Rome's interests, for example ensuring Rome's grain supply. Here beginneth the Roman Empire.

But this was not the result of any far-sighted plan. As has been pointed out, power in the ancient world depended on mastering natural resources. As soon as you had mastered them, you wanted to keep them, and you could do that securely only by mastering *more* of them – as need directed (p. 1).

218–201 BC: THE SECOND PUNIC WAR

After its defeat in the First Punic War, Carthage realized that if it was to retain its dominance in the western Mediterranean, it had to act fast. Rome had imposed a gigantic indemnity on it (3,200 talents of silver = 183,000 pounds in weight), and inflation was rampant. The Carthaginians therefore looked to Spain, with its phenomenally rich silver mines, to restore their fortunes.

Under Hamilcar Barca, his son Hannibal and brother Hasdrubal, southern Spain was brought under Carthaginian control.

WHAT'S IN A NAME?

Hannibal was the Roman form of Chenu Ba'al, meaning 'loved by Baal', the ferocious Old Testament god. The surname Barca survives in the name Barcelona.

When war with Rome was declared, Hannibal left his brother Hasdrubal in charge of Spain and prepared to take the fight to the enemy. Carthage no longer being master of the sea, he began his long and famous march, with elephants, up through Spain, across Gaul, over the Alps and down into Italy.

HANNIBAL, MASTER TACTICIAN

Hannibal's strategy was to win over Rome's allies by the threat he could pose to them. His military tactics? The *unexpected*: that meant surprise – ambush and attack from the sides or the rear, rather than the usual full-on frontal assault.

His first meeting with the Romans at the Trebia river left 30,000 Roman soldier-*plebs* dead; his next, at Lake Trasimene – an ambush – 15,000 dead and 15,000 captured. Locals were so confident he would win that they followed the army, keen to pick up booty after the battle.

But at that stage none of Rome's allies in central Italy were won over to Carthage's side. Moreover, Rome sent an army under Publius Cornelius Scipio and his brother Gnaeus Scipio by sea direct to Spain, to take on Carthage there and prevent reinforcements being sent to Hannibal. They enjoyed a great deal of success against the scattered Carthaginian forces.

218 BC: A LAW AGAINST SENATORIAL TRADING

Senators were not supposed to engage in trading. It was said to be beneath them; they should be busy looking after the state and their own extensive lands in the interests of the *plebs*. A tribune, Claudius, proposed a measure to turn this into law – making it illegal for a senator, or his son, to possess any sea-going vessel that would hold more than 300 amphoras (one amphora held about six gallons) of wine. The opposition to this proposal from the senatorial rank was ferocious, while the *plebs* gave it their full support. The law was passed and the consul Flaminius was the only senator to support it. As a result, he won a second term of office.

Rome's response to Hannibal's devastating victories was left to the dictator Fabius Maximus *Cunctator* ('the delayer'). He was given that nickname because, after Hannibal's stunning successes, he decided that the best thing to do was not to engage with Hannibal but instead to track him and harry him. This forced Hannibal to think about where he and his troops could winter, since the territory of Falernus, where he was currently stationed, 'with its fruit-trees, vineyards and other produce that was agreeable rather than necessary offered only seasonal, not permanent supplies'.

216 BC: THE BATTLE OF CANNAE

Despite Fabius demonstrating that his tactics were successful, many were unhappy with them, and it was decided to fight Hannibal at

Cannae. The consul Lucius Aemilius Paullus was joined as consul by the brash Gaius Varro – Livy said they got on as well as two gladiators facing each other in the circus – to take on Hannibal in open combat.

GAIUS VARRO, THE BUTCHER

Gaius Varro came from a humble background. The son of a butcher, who retailed his own meat and brought his son into the business, Varro inherited his father's money and developed political ambitions, taking up a sequence of official positions in the hope of becoming consul. To achieve that, he decided to support the *plebs*.

Thanks to a foolish assault by the inexperienced Varro, the Romans were slaughtered at Cannae, losing something in the region of 50,000 *plebs* while 17,000 surrendered. Paullus was killed, but Varro took charge of the retreat to Venusia, whose *plebs* rallied round them, finding them billets, clothing and cash.

At this point, many Roman allies, including the Samnites and Campanians, many Greek settlements to the south of Italy, and all the Gauls on the other side of the Alps moved over to the Carthaginian side.

TAKING THE LONG VIEW

Cannae was a great victory for Hannibal, but it was very difficult to secure the loyalty of those cities he had won in that part of Italy, which confined him largely to southern Italy and unable to attack the north. Carthage was thinking hard about how it could help, but decided that retaking Sicily from the Romans would be a good idea: it was perfect as a secure launchpad for a seaborne assault.

The Romans were well aware that, sooner or later, Hannibal would be reinforced. That was why they had sent the two Scipios to take on Carthage in Spain. When they were defeated and killed in 211 BC, Rome sent out another army under Publius' son (*the* Scipio Africanus – aged twenty-five!) – to take the fight to Hasdrubal and Hamilcar, Hannibal's generals in Spain. It says much for Roman thinking that, for all the military disasters in Italy, they could still look dispassionately at the broader picture of how things might go and react to it.

That meant enlisting *plebs* under the age of eighteen into the army. Likewise, at a time when Rome had previously refused to enlist free *plebs* who had no property (p. 150), even slaves (some 24,000) were bought from their owners with public money (by a vote of the *plebs*) and drafted into the army, as both foot soldiers and cavalry, 'many taken from slave lodgings and... gathered from shepherd huts'.

PLEB POWER

Two crooked tax collectors, Postumius and Titus, were taking advantage of a ruling that during times of war the state would pay for any ships lost at sea while carrying goods to armies. They bought some rotten hulks with valueless cargoes, sank them and reported the loss, enormously exaggerating the value. The Senate, knowing that the state was short of money but desperately needing all the tax it could collect, refused to take action because they did not want to make enemies of the tax collectors.

But the *plebs* were made of sterner stuff. They imposed a huge fine on Postumius, which was appealed, and on the day of the trial the tribune Casca (a relative of Postumius) attempted to veto the whole procedure. The accused tried to escape, the trial was ended, and the Senate met to decide what to do with the tax collectors and their supporters. The decision was handed over to the *plebs*, who sent the main culprits to prison while other supporters went into exile.

210 BC: THE YOUTH OF ROME

The *plebs* were now thoroughly involved in making decisions about who should lead their armies, and on one occasion, at a critical moment in the war, a group consisting of younger voters appointed a well-known general, who regretfully told them that he was no longer fit enough to do the job. The younger voters immediately consulted the senior voters, to whose suggestion they deferred.

Writing in the first century BC, Livy comments that such deference would be unthinkable in his own time: 'If there were a city composed of wise men of the sort that the learned have imagined in some ideal world, I cannot think it would contain leaders with a greater sense of serious purpose and less lust for personal power, or a people of more admirable character. It may seem simply incredible that a group of younger voters should consult their seniors about whom to entrust with power. But that is down to the fact that, in our day, even the authority of parents over their children is held cheap and of little account.'

FUNDING THE FLEET

Given Rome's concern about a possible reinforcement of Hannibal by the Carthaginian fleet, the call went out to man the Roman fleet, but there was not enough money to pay the recruits. The consuls then called on private individuals, according to their financial status, to provide oarsmen with pay and provisions for thirty days.

That was greeted with a roar of protests from the *plebs*: crowds surrounded the consuls, arguing that they had already been drained dry by taxation; the enemy had burned down their homes, and the state had stolen their slaves to turn them into oarsman or soldiers.

The consuls gave up and the next day called a meeting of the Senate to decide what to do. The senators decided that *they themselves* would fund the whole operation. They would bring all their gold, silver, and bronze coin, keeping a certain amount back for themselves, and place it in the treasury.

The senators did this with such enthusiasm that the clerks could hardly keep up with recording who had paid what! The next wealthiest group, the *equites*, then paid up what they could, followed by the remaining *plebs*, and the job was done.

209 BC: APPOINTING A DICTATOR AND A PRIEST

The Romans decided to appoint as dictator Valerius Messalla to ensure that the fleet could be built and take control of its operation. But could a dictator be appointed to serve *outside* Italy? A plebeian tribune put the question to the Senate, which decreed that the *plebs*, surprisingly, should make the choice. Which they did, but appointing Quintus Fulvius instead.

The question then arose of an important priesthood, which up until then had gone automatically to a patrician. Atellus, a plebeian, had put himself forward but had been rejected by the patricians. The tribunes referred the matter to the Senate, who again referred it back to the *plebs*, and Atellus was duly appointed.

Both these examples demonstrate how much the distinction between *plebs* and patricians was losing its significance.

207 BC: HASDRUBAL'S FAILURE

In Spain, Scipio Africanus reverted to the attacking strategy of his dead father and uncle. By the end of the year, Carthage had lost its Spanish possessions forever.

Hasdrubal's army had left Spain to join Hannibal in Italy. But by a stroke of luck, the Romans learned where Hasdrubal and Hannibal were planning to meet. The outnumbered Hasdrubal was defeated and Hannibal learned what had happened when his brother's head was hurled into his camp. He withdrew into the mountains of Italy's toe and stayed there, without emerging, for another four years.

205 BC: TAKING THE WAR TO CARTHAGE

Fresh from his Spanish victories, Scipio was elected consul and asked the Senate for permission to take the war from Spain into North Africa and attack Carthage directly. The senators were very reluctant, since they still were worried about Hannibal's continued presence in Italy and were anxious not to impose further burdens on the allied towns. But when Scipio appealed over their heads to the Plebeian Assembly, promising vengeance on the Carthaginians for all the sufferings they had inflicted on the *plebs*, the Senate gave way, somewhat grudgingly.

Scipio brought his total army up to 30,000 *plebs*; and with this force he landed in North Africa some twenty miles from Carthage. There he was joined by a neighbouring prince, Masinissa, king of part of Numidia (eastern Algeria), who had changed sides and brought with him a superb cavalry.

203–202 BC: HANNIBAL RETURNS HOME

In 203 BC Hannibal was recalled from Italy, his fifteen-year-long invasion at an end. He boasted of having destroyed 400 towns and killing 300,000 soldier-*plebs*. By now, Carthage had begun negotiations for peace with the Romans and the discussions had reached an advanced stage, but Hannibal persuaded his government to break the talks off.

At that, Scipio moved inland to sever Carthage from its agricultural supplies, and in 202 BC, near Zama, seventy-five miles from the city, the final battle of the war was fought, and Hannibal was defeated.

And who was it who was asked to decide whether to continue the war or end it – and if ending it, to ratify the peace and bring the army back from Africa? The answer was the *plebs*, who voted to end the war and order Scipio, the great hero of the whole victory, to ratify the victory and bring the army home.

In the final analysis, it was sheer Roman manpower that beat Hannibal – and it was *plebs*, under fine leadership, who had done the fighting.

Spain was then turned into two provinces.

THE DEATH OF HANNIBAL

Hannibal spent the rest of his life on the move, playing politics around the eastern Mediterranean, finally ending up in Bithynia (northern Turkey) under the hospitality of King Prusias. The Romans got wind of this and asked Prusias where Hannibal was. Prusias did not tell them but simply said, 'Seek and ye shall find.' So the Romans did, and located him in a castle built with many escape routes. When a slave told Hannibal that he could see an army approaching, Hannibal realized it was all up with him and 'not wanting to put his life at anyone else's disposal, he took the vial of poison he always kept with him and, calling up his ancient valour, drained it dry'.

146 BC: CARTHAGE OBLITERATED

Various treaties and agreements were arranged with Carthage, but none of them held. The old Roman, Cato the Elder, who kept on repeating in the Senate, 'Carthage must be destroyed', finally got his way – and in the Third Punic War, after a long siege, the city was wiped off the map, its buildings destroyed and thrown down the sides of the hill on which Carthage was poised.

CARTHAGE SOWN WITH SALT?

That idea that Carthage was sown with salt after its defeat was put forward in the nineteenth century and published in a scholarly book in 1930. But there is not one iota of evidence for it. Romans were not stupid. Why on earth destroy the agricultural productivity of a city in a magnificent location that they now owned?

Rome made North Africa a province and opened it up to farming; and a hundred years later, under Julius Caesar and Augustus, a new colony was founded there. It was the start of a golden era that was to see Carthage as the capital of North Africa, with a population of 300,000 at its peak – a city of the highest importance in the Roman Empire, and the later Christian world.

THE GREEK ADVENTURE: 197–146 BC

You will probably not be surprised to learn that, while all this was going on, Rome was also engaged in yet *another* war – in Greece. Its main player at this time was the powerful Philip V, king of

Macedonia, i.e. Greece under Macedonian control. After the Roman defeat at Cannae in 216 BC, Philip signed a peace agreement with Carthage, hoping to benefit from Rome's defeat, but nothing came of it.

After their victory over Hannibal in 202 BC, the Romans got their own back. They returned to Greece and conquered Philip in 197 BC, informing all the Greeks that they were now 'free', i.e. part of the Roman Empire (!) – and they had better understand it, right?

Not surprisingly, this did not go down well with the freedom-loving Greeks, and when Philip died his son (now King) Perseus decided it was time to drive out their Roman overlords. In 171 BC, he declared war.

A LOYAL PLEB-SOLDIER

The Romans at once began enlisting men for the fight against Perseus, and many *plebs* were keen to join up 'because those who had served there before had become rich'. It was decided to enlist no one above the age of fifty-one. But some of the *plebs* who had served earlier and reached the position of chief centurion found themselves appointed to the ordinary ranks.

At that point, one of them was given permission to say a few words before the assembly of *plebs* who were witnessing the whole procedure:

> Citizens of Rome, I am Spurius Ligustinus, of the clan
> Crustumena, and I come of Sabine stock. My father left me
> half an acre of land and the little hut in which I was born and

brought up. I am still living there today. As soon as I came
of age, my father gave me his brother's daughter to wife, who
brought nothing with her save her free birth and her chastity,
together with a fertility which would be enough even for a
wealthy home. We have six sons, and two daughters (both
already married). Four of my sons have taken the toga of
manhood; two are still underage.

Spurius then described how he had served on and off for
twenty-two years and was now over fifty. He had been awarded
thirty-four military decorations, including six civic crowns (the
highest decoration). He had been chief centurion four times. He
admitted his age was against him, but he did not care what rank he
was given; he just wanted to serve, come what may, and suggested
that those other ex-chief centurions should take the same view.
Spurius got his wish, and the others fell into line.

One could make a shrewd guess that Spurius, given his record,
had been very well rewarded indeed for his military efforts so far,
and had made the judgement that he was about to do even better. If
so, his judgement turned out to be absolutely correct.

GREECE: A ROMAN PROVINCE

Perseus enjoyed some early successes, but the Roman army under
Aemilius Paullus was not to be denied. On 22 June 168 BC, the
Roman army won the day. But wars continued on and off until
146 BC, when Macedonia and the rest of Greece were turned into
a Roman province.

To make the point – perhaps because of some anti-Roman action we do not know about – the Romans not only defeated the fabulously wealthy Greek city of Corinth and looted it of its magnificent artworks, but also burned it to the ground.

Livy's history of Rome from 167 BC has been lost, bar odd quotes and fragments.

THE CLUE TO ROME'S SUCCESS: A GREEK VIEW

In 167 BC, Rome had taken 1,000 Greek hostages to try to secure the peace against Macedonia. The Greek diplomat Polybius was one of them.

Polybius was soon mixing with the Roman great and good and was especially fascinated by the republican system, which seemed so secure and so successful – something of a contrast to the volatile democratic Greek world in which he had grown up.

He put it down to the balance that the Romans seemed to have been able to generate between men who had competing interests: those in favour of rule by monarchs; those in favour of the rule of an oligarchy, i.e. a select few; and those in favour of democracy, the rule of the many.

He saw those three interests exemplified in the consuls, each one acting as a head of state for a year and holding absolute military power; the Senate, a select few, originating in membership restricted to the rank of patricians, who were in charge of expenditure and revenue; and the *plebs*, who over time gained the right to pass laws, and controlled the courts (for capital offences) and the election to public offices.

This system, he thought, gave Romans a sense of unity and purpose that enabled them to do whatever they wanted to – but most important of all, to stand unbreakably together when danger threatened. Each coalition consented to the roles of the others and felt an obligation to work with and maintain them.

POLYBIUS ON ITALY

Polybius was also deeply impressed by the fertility of Italy. He commented on the cheapness of corn, barley and other grains, wine and acorns, which 'feed the huge number of pigs slaughtered every year for domestic consumption and to feed the army'. The cheapness and sheer quantity of food available was illustrated by travellers in the region. When they arrived at an inn, they did not haggle over the price but simply asked what it was per head for board and lodging. The innkeepers would provide an inclusive tariff and rarely charged more than that.

IX

FROM TRIUMPH TO DISASTER:

167–27 BC

THE TRIUMPH

The wealth that the Romans brought home from that campaign in Greece was staggering. For the troops, plundering the homes of the rich – whether they were allowed to or not – would have provided very happy hunting grounds. Together with the subsequent share of booty, these spoils certainly made many of them far better off than they had ever been before.

But for the wealthy, educated, elite upper ranks of the military, it would have been like having Venice, the British Museum and the vaults of the Bank of England open from which to take their pick.

They seized statues and artworks in vast quantities to bring back to their homes, to show off their achievements and their good taste in art (inventing the idea of 'art collecting', though something similar had already happened in 264 BC when a Roman general took 2,000 statues from Volsinii in Etruria!). Few Romans at home would have seen stuff like that in their whole lives.

Here, then, is the Greek historian Appian's description of the booty that Aemilius Paullus brought home to Rome after the defeat of King Perseus. The enthusiasm of the *plebs* to get a good sight of the show is transparent:

The *plebs* put up scaffolding in the Forum, in the Circus Maximus and other racing circuits, and in all other parts of the city where they could get a good view. The roads were cleared and kept open by teams of officials who restrained those crowding onto or running across the main avenue. This triumph lasted three days.

On the first day, which was scarcely long enough to see everything that was on view, the statues, pictures, and colossal images taken from the enemy were pulled through the city by two hundred and fifty chariots.

On the second day was carried, in a great many carts, the finest and richest armour of the Macedonians, both of brass and steel, all newly polished and glittering, fastened together so loosely that it banged together with a terrifying noise.

After these came carts loaded with armour followed by three thousand men carrying coined silver weighing 200 kilos in seven hundred and fifty vessels, each of which was carried by four men. Others brought silver bowls and goblets and cups, all exciting curiosity for their size and the solidity of their embossed work.

On the third day, early in the morning, first came trumpeters sounding a charge that the Romans use when they spur on the soldiers to fight. Next followed young men leading to the sacrifice of a hundred and twenty oxen, with their horns gilded, and their heads adorned with ribbons and garlands; and with these were boys carrying silver and gold basins for libations.

After this were brought 77 vessels full of gold coin, each weighing 200 kilos.* These were followed by men bringing the consecrated bowl which Aemilius had ordered to be made, set with precious stones and weighing 700 kilos. Then were displayed the cups of the Macedonian Kings Antigonus and Seleucus, and all the gold plate that was used at Perseus' table. Next to these came Perseus' chariot, in which his armour was placed, and on that his diadem.

All this was paraded before the eyes of the Roman *plebs*, many of whom must have fought in the battles that seized this unbelievable wealth. Surely the overriding reaction must have been: '*We* did this. It's all *our* work. What it is to be Roman!' It is hard to imagine they did not say to themselves, proudly, that it had all been worth it.

At the same time, the crowd was not oblivious to the plight of the losers, especially the children. When Perseus' chariot had passed:

After a brief interval, came the children of the King, led along as slaves… two boys, and one girl, not really aware of the magnitude of their evils because of their tender youth. As a

---

* The current price of gold (June 2025) is £80,000 per kilo, of silver £863 per kilo.

result, they evoked even more pity, because in time they would realize what had happened to them; and while Perseus walked along almost unheeded, the Romans, moved by compassion, fixed their eyes on the children, many shedding tears, and for all of them their delight in the spectacle was mixed with anguish, until the children had passed by.

Hardened *plebs* knew all too well what was likely to happen to the children of their enemies.

GREEKIFICATION

This had an enormous influence upon the rich in Rome. All things Greek – philosophy, literature, art, architecture – became fashionable, much to the horror of 'good old Romans' like Cato the Elder, who publicly inveighed against its corrupting influence (though he did actually learn Greek himself).

Meanwhile, the Greeks were not slow to see the opportunities this brought about. Philosophers, teachers, artists, doctors, poets, craftsmen and architects all flooded into Rome, offering their services for sale. Soon the sons of the elite were being educated in Greek; Romans dressed as Greeks and held Greek-style drinking parties (*symposia*).

Roman writers also began creatively drawing upon the works of the ancient Greek masters, producing what would turn out to be a unique and enormously influential literature of their own – from epics and love poetry to philosophy (especially Stoicism and Epicureanism) and works on politics, history and so on.

It was a massive cultural and artistic revolution for this clan of fighting farmers. The result was, as the Roman poet Horace put it, 'Conquered Greece took rustic Rome captive and introduced culture to countrymen speaking – Latin!'

Rome with its provinces was now the dominant power in the Mediterranean. The wealth that the Romans had accrued was monumental – so much so that in 167 BC they gave up collecting income tax in Rome. Wealth created wealth and almost unlimited opportunity for investment, financial dealings and business.

THE MILITARY IMPLICATIONS

Rome's lengthy battles with Carthage and the Greeks also created an important change in the Roman mentality. Costly and exhausting they may have been, but the wars were won and Rome's control over wealthy territory was enormously extended. These victories opened Roman eyes to what could be done, with the *plebs* now thoroughly accustomed to spending long periods abroad and, like Spurius Ligustinus, well aware of the rewards that beckoned.

Over the next hundred years, despite the political chaos that ruled in Rome, Pompey had by 64 BC turned the Greek world east as far as Syria into a Roman province, quadrupling Rome's income, and Julius Caesar conquered Gaul by 50 BC (having sniffed around Britain in 55 and 54 BC). There would be more to come.

BUT WHAT NEXT FOR THE PLEBS?

The historian Appian described Rome's Italian conquests over the next two centuries as follows: 'As the Romans conquered Italian peoples, they would build towns on the land they seized, or move colonists into those already existing, to use them as outposts; and they handed over to colonists, or sold or leased, the cultivated land.'

That was the 'public land' that Rome acquired as it fought its way down Italy: it was carved up into lots and distributed among the poorer *plebs* to help solve the problems of poverty.

But everyone, and especially the wealthy among them, knew that wealth lay in land. Now that they had made vast fortunes from the recent wars of conquest in Carthage and the East, what better way to invest it than in more land? And why not work it with slaves, since so many had been captured during the wars?

Meanwhile, those *plebs* whose service in the military proved to be a blessing – all that booty! – might well have been able to add to their farms or improve efficiency with more slaves.

The net result of this was an increase in social mobility among many in the Roman world, but at the cost of those who had not been so fortunate and were forced to sell their land and work it for its new owners (unless they were replaced by slaves). For them, the consequences were to be catastrophic.

133–132 BC: TIBERIUS GRACCHUS' REFORMS

Tiberius Gracchus, via his mother Cornelia, was the grandson of Scipio Africanus. Not the sort of person who, one might imagine, would want to mix it with the *plebs*, but he can be seen as a reformer, who saw a way to power by doing something about the plight of *plebs* who owned no land – or who'd had to sell it because of debt.

LIFE ON THE STREET IN ROME

For perjurers, try the Comitium. Liars and braggarts hang around the shrine of Cloacina: rich, married ne'er do wells by the Basilica. Packs of prostitutes there too, but rather clapped-out ones. In the Fish Market, members of dining clubs. In the Lower Forum, respectable well-to-do citizens out for a stroll; in the Middle Forum, flashier types, along the canal. By the Lacus Curtius, you'll find bold fellows with a tongue in their head and evil thoughts in their mind, great slanderers of others, and very vulnerable to it themselves. By the Old Shops the moneylenders – they'll make or take a loan. Behind the temple of Castor, there are men to whom you wouldn't trust yourself. In the Vicus Tuscus are men who sell themselves. In the Velabrum, you'll find a baker or a butcher or a fortune teller – or men who will do a turn for you or get you to do a turn for them.

In the eyes of the early comic poet Plautus (d. 184 BC)

On gaining the trust of the plebs, Tiberius became a plebeian (!) tribune in 133 BC and laid a bill before the Plebeian Assembly. Its subject was those Italian cities which had been given land by the Romans, but during the second Carthaginian war had gone over to Hannibal. It proposed that their land should be taken and parcelled out among poor Roman *plebs*. At the same time, no one should be able to own more than 500 *iugera* of public land bought during war. The Senate, most of whom who would be hit hard by the latter part of this bill, tried to block it by refusing to pay for its enactment.

But the kingdom of the Greek monarch Attalus III (western Turkey) had just been bequeathed to Rome, and Tiberius proposed another bill to use finance from that source to fund the new land settlement. When Tiberius stood for the tribunate a second time in 132 BC, a mob of senators led by Rome's high priest clubbed him and many of his supporters to death.

132–44 BC: FACTIONAL STRIFE AND CIVIL WAR

In all the years of Rome's political battles between patricians and *plebs*, such conflict was unprecedented, and it proved a turning point, driving a wedge between those in favour of the reforms (the pro-plebeian *populares*), and those against (the pro-senator *optimates*). Here we go again.

But at least Tiberius' reforms were partly implemented.

96 BC: MISPLACED IRONY?

The censors expelled Duronius from the Senate, because when he was tribune of the *plebs* he had vetoed a law that had been introduced to restrict spending on banquets. The remarkable reason for his expulsion was that he had made the following public speech in the Forum: 'A bridle has been forced upon you that cannot be endured in any way. You have been bound and restricted by the bitter chains of slavery; a law has been proposed that commands you to be frugal! Let us veto this law that is covered with the rust of the harsh old days. What is the point of freedom if you cannot ruin yourselves in luxury when you want to?'

Valerius Maximus

91–87 BC: THE SOCIAL WAR

But while factional strife between these two groups continued, a conflict between Rome and its Italian allies broke out. Called the Social War, it was triggered by issues that dominated the *plebs'* recent fight for power:

- Denial of citizenship to many Italian cities that provided manpower for the Roman army and paid taxes, but otherwise had no political say;

- The distribution of land favouring Roman citizens, leaving Italians landless;

- The assassination of Marcus Livius Drusus, a tribune who backed citizenship for Italians;

- General dissatisfaction at being under Rome's thumb.

The most significant result of the Social War was that the Romans compromised, increasing citizenship – according to a full census of 70 BC – by about a million. Not that all the new Romano-Italian citizens moved into Rome (!), but they could now play a part in Roman politics – as many as wanted to, that is, and as had the time and money and interest to attend the assemblies in Rome.

POSTAL VOTING

The emperor Augustus (27 BC – AD 14) toyed with the idea of a system of postal voting, at least to allow the Italian senators in every enfranchised town to have a say 'whereby the members of the Senate in each colony cast their votes for magistracies in the capital and then sent them under seal to Rome in time for the elections', according to Suetonius in his *Life of Augustus*. But the idea was not pursued.

The implications of this massive extension of the franchise will be pursued shortly.

88–49 BC: CIVIL WARS

No sooner had the Social War finished than the factional strife that had characterized Roman political life since the time of Tiberius Gracchus turned into open warfare. The two generals Marius (*popularis*) and Sulla (*optimate*) used their enormous wealth to raise and train private armies to fight it out in three major conflicts between 88 and 81 BC, with Sulla emerging as the victor (he died in 78 BC). The defeated *popularis* forces retreated to Spain and held out until 72 BC, when they were finally defeated by the *optimate* Pompey.

Pompey was an outstanding general and consequently was the first choice of the Roman *plebs* to rid the Mediterranean of piracy

– which he did in three months (in 67 BC) – and then to sort out Mithradates, of Greek and Persian ancestry, who was the ruthless ruler of Pontus. This was an area east of the Black Sea, stretching from eastern Turkey to Odessa, which he expanded to cover all of Asia Minor (western Turkey). He had ambitions to destroy Rome's interests there and in Greece.

Not only did Pompey deal with Mithradates (66–63 BC), he at the same time extended Roman power as far as Syria, enormously increasing Rome's revenue from the provinces.

The Senate was terrified that, when he returned, Pompey would take over Rome himself, but what he did instead was form an alliance with Julius Caesar and the richest man in Rome, Marcus Licinius Crassus (the three of them making up a triumvirate), to control Rome in their own interests. The republic descended into lawlessness – intimidation and assassination, street-fighting and the disruption of elections.

On Crassus' death in 53 BC, Pompey aligned himself with the Senate against Caesar who since 59 BC had been busy conquering Gaul. In 52 BC he was made sole consul in an effort to restore order. When the *popularis* Caesar completed his successful ten-year campaign in Gaul and demanded that he be allowed to return to Rome prosecution-free – he knew his enemies had it in for him – it was civil war. Caesar defeated Pompey in 49 BC and made himself dictator for life, only to be assassinated on the Ides (15th) of March in 44 BC.

CUI BONO?

Cicero tells us this question originated in 137 BC, when the judge Cassius was always instructing the jurors in any trial to ask (literally) 'To whom [was it for] an advantage?' – i.e. 'Who stood to gain?'

44–27 BC: FROM CAESAR TO AUGUSTUS

An uneasy peace and then further civil war between Caesar's heir, the nineteen-year-old Octavian, and Caesar's previous close ally Marc Antony, supported by Cleopatra, concluded in 31 BC with victory for Octavian. In 27 BC he renamed himself Augustus, calling himself not 'emperor' – as bad as 'king' for any freedom-loving Roman to accept – but *princeps* (compare 'principal'), meaning 'first citizen'.

He became the first in a line of anything between seventy and eighty emperors (depending how you count). The empire technically ended in AD 476, though some consider that it re-emerged as the Holy Roman Empire in 1254 and lasted until its final 'heir' Francis II abdicated in 1806 to become emperor of Austria – how are the mighty fallen! – as Francis I.

AN IMPERIAL PLEB

Augustus was born in 63 BC into a wealthy plebeian family of cavalryman status (*equites*, p. 26). In 47 BC Caesar enrolled him as a patrician and adopted him but, when he became emperor, Augustus thought it wiser to present himself as a *pleb*.

PLEBS AT WAR

And where were the *plebs* in all this? As usual, fighting battles, but this time against each other, in the interests of the Roman elites to whom they had allied themselves. Perhaps around 100,000 *plebs* were killed in the (un)civil wars between 88 BC and 31 BC, in addition to around 9,000 members of the elites on the 'wrong' side at any stage, whose property was also seized.

FREEDOM, FAREWELL?

One result of this political earthquake was that the *plebs'* say in political power in Rome, which they had worked so hard to win, was now at an end. All the Assemblies were dissolved by the second emperor, Tiberius, in AD 17, and their powers transferred to the Senate whose membership Tiberius called 'men fit to be slaves'. There was no comeback from the *plebs*, who would no more argue with the emperor than they would with the dictator...

X

THE AUGUSTAN REVOLUTION:

AN OVERVIEW

But the plebeian loss of rights was as nothing compared with the much larger earthquake created by the internal *optimate-popularis* conflicts of the last 110 years, from Tiberius Gracchus' reforms to Augustus' Principate. As we have already seen, the ancient Roman patrician vs. *plebs* conflict had long been resolved, but the old noble families that had once ruled the roost were finding the ground shifting under their feet in the new political alignment. The massive influx of a million new citizens as a result of the Social War finally helped to end the grip of those families on the political scene, and opened up opportunities and influence to others with political and commercial interests – especially the *equites*, who were the second wealthiest group after the patricians.

This trend is neatly exemplified in the speeches of the statesman and philosopher Cicero (d. 44 BC), a member of the old guard if ever there was one, even though he was a *novus homo*, 'new man', i.e. the first member of his family ever to be a consul! Well aware of what was happening, he regularly contrasted the country existence of the 'real' old Roman patrician, quietly living a life of honest effort, frugality and justice off his thousands of acres of land, with what he saw as the new Roman, characterized by his sheer avarice, no longer interested in the old ways but rather desperate to show off his status by embarrassing displays of wealth, and driven by greed into all sorts of dodgy dealings. It hinted at the end of the old order.

ORDER, ORDER

Order was a concept of which the Romans were much in favour. The word derives from the Latin *ordo* (stem *ordin-*), which originally meant a thread on a loom and then a row of something, for example seats at the games. The word went on to mean 'a rank, standing, position, class, order of succession', all suggesting rules and structures, part of that endless search for perfect systems. There was a new *ordo* in Rome, but how perfect would remain to be seen...

Meanwhile, the fantastic wealth that had accrued and was still accruing from Rome's empire was all placed in the lap of the Roman emperor himself. This now included the fabulous riches of Egypt, which had been the domain of Marc Antony but which at the end of the civil war Augustus had turned into a province under his own personal control.

That wealth, combined with the massive political and social shift, was to have profound consequences for the Roman world.

And perhaps the most dramatic was Augustus's reorganization of the state.

THE POOR: A SNAPSHOT

As Jesus said, the poor you have with you always. It is best to be reminded of that so that one can bear it in mind as the rather more optimistic picture presented by the Augustan revolution unfolds.

The great majority of the *plebs* were peasant farmers. All things, especially the weather, being equal, they would have been the lucky ones – some with large farms, very lucky. But at the poorer end of the *plebs*, life in the city is rather well summarized in this funerary inscription: 'All a person needs. Bones reposing sweetly, I am not anxious about suddenly being short of food. I do not suffer from arthritis, and I am not indebted because of being behind in my rent. In fact, my lodgings are permanent – and free!'

Security at last! Although no Roman ever said that wealth was a 'good' or a form of virtue, money was the difference between life and death. Only a multi-millionaire like Seneca (adviser to Nero, which cost him his life) could argue that what you have is irrelevant, since what you do not have amounts to so much more. But for the destitute, whose only 'home' was the protection provided by the vast, elaborate tombs of the great and the good – though there was a law forbidding people to seek shelter there – an early death was their inevitable fate. That is why we know so little about them.

In the city, accommodation always created problems. It was rented, and expensive and of mixed classes: often rich and poor lived side by side, shack next to palace. Overcrowding and violence were commonplace. The historian Suetonius tells us that the emperor Augustus enjoyed watching groups of *plebs* brawling in narrow city streets. A legal text tells us of a shopkeeper putting his lantern out on the pavement. A passer-by grabbed it and the shopkeeper gave chase. The thief hit him with a lash, and in the brawl the shopkeeper knocked out one of the thief's eyes. No police to sort it out, of course: that would be a commission for the praetor (p. 49) or 'friends'.

Even when work was obtained, it was often organized on short-term contracts, especially if it was taken during the harvest and vintage. We hear of a woman who gave birth while working on a day-contract in a digging gang. Fearful of losing her wages, she hid the child and carried on. She was spotted and, against all expectations, paid in full and sent home by a kindly manager.

The fact is that many *plebs* had to do anything to make money. There were, for example, street performers such as the *circulator*, who addressed a *circulus* of willing listeners. There are accounts of them outside the Circus Maximus, all doing what they hoped would attract a few coins from the crowd: dancing, playing the flute, reading a poem, singing, telling a story or myth, performing a trick.

The job of the *stercorarius* (or night-soil man, as he was known well into the 1950s in Britain) was to empty the cesspits and sell the contents to farmers on the city outskirts. Assume that the average Roman generated about one and half pounds of body waste a day. Late imperial Rome, if its population really did reach a million, would therefore have generated about 500 tons of daily sewage. Plenty of work there.

The satirical novelist Petronius (d. c. AD 66) describes the 'heroes' of his story moving on to the next town and picking someone up off the streets to carry their luggage for them:

> He complained constantly about the job and kept putting down our luggage and cursing us for walking too fast and swearing that he would either throw our luggage away or run off with all of it. 'What do you think I am?' he said. 'A pack animal or a cargo ship? I hired myself out to do the work of a man, not a horse! I'm no less a free man than you people, even if my father did leave me a pauper.' And not content with swearing at us, he immediately lifted up his leg and filled the street with the noise and odour of a fart.

Augustus' revolution did nothing for those in such situations. But what it appears to have done is created more opportunities for those able to take them.

AUGUSTUS: REORGANIZING THE STATE

First, as has already been observed (p. 194), under Augustus, governance shifted from relying on the usual suspects – old chums among the nobles and Senate – to employing more 'professional' *equites*, educated *plebs* and even freedmen in highly responsible, top-end administrative roles, most put in place by the emperor himself. They took charge of key functions such as finance, administration, legal affairs and public works, forming an organized bureaucracy that would expand under later emperors. The famous old families of the republic were out. The republican apparatus still existed – Senate, consuls and so on – but these were shadows of their former selves.

AUGUSTUS AND THE *PLEBS*

A man who had been struck by a stone on active service and had an obvious, unsightly scar on his forehead, was bragging loudly of his exploits and received this gentle rebuke from Augustus: 'Never look round when you are running away.'

Macrobius , c. AD 400

Even more dramatically, Augustus also set about solving the problem of the wealthy using money to raise their own private armies (as he himself had done!) to win power. He did so by turning military service into a properly state-funded profession, paid for with a 5 per cent tax on inheritances and bequests. In other words, the whole concept of the 'career' was invented for the army and, to some extent, for the administration as well.

Here, then, was Rome's first standing army, protecting Rome's empire, each province of which was ruled by a governor. The military also acted as local peacekeepers and builders of infra-structure, especially roads designed to ease the movement of troops and imperial messengers. Soldiers enjoyed regular pay, conditions, prospects of promotion, and a pension plus bonus. The army's loyalty was now tied to the emperor and no one else. By AD 211, it numbered 450,000. The most privileged unit was the Praetorian Guard, based in Rome, which both guarded and acted as the ears and eyes of the emperor.

It must be said that this did not solve the problem of rebellious soldiers. For example, in AD 68 Rome's legions in Germany rebelled against Nero and he committed suicide. Since he was the last of Augustus' extended family, there was no natural successor, and in AD 69, the 'Year of the Four Emperors', the governors of Spain (Galba), Lusitania (Otho), Lower Germany (Vitellius) and Judea (Vespasian) marched on Rome to fight it out for the prize with Vespasian emerging as emperor on 21 December. Such insurgencies became fairly common in the late Roman Empire.

But one result of Augustus professionalizing the army was that even more of the power of the old guard slipped away: they were no longer the top generals. With the Senate largely yes-men, power was now devolved to Augustus' personal 'court' and political life became something of a charade.

AUGUSTUS: AN ALTERNATIVE VIEW

The great Roman historian Tacitus despised the emperors as the equivalent of kings.

> He seduced the army with bonuses, and his cheap food policy was successful bait for civilians. Indeed, he attracted everybody's goodwill by the enjoyable gift of peace. Then

he gradually pushed ahead and absorbed the functions of the Senate, the officials, and even the law. Opposition did not exist. War or judicial murder had disposed of all men of spirit. Upper class survivors found that slavish obedience was the way to succeed both politically and financially. They had profited from the revolution, and so they now liked the security of the existing arrangements better than the dangerous uncertainties of the old regime.

Tacitus, *Annals* 1.1, composed c. AD 110

Not, of course, that Augustus could possibly have seen it like that. He was well aware of the Roman love of tradition, the old ways of doing things, which were by definition much better than modern ways. (It is no coincidence that the Latin for 'ancestors' was *maiores*, meaning 'greater' – from which we get our word 'major'.) He argued that, after the horrors of the civil wars, his 'revolution' was a restoration of the 'greater days'.

AUGUSTUS AND THE *PLEBS*

Augustus was approached by Herennius, a young man of bad character who had committed an offence and been dismissed from the army. He asked Augustus, 'How will I explain this to my father?' Augustus replied, 'Tell your father that you didn't find me to your liking.'

Macrobius

AUGUSTUS' BENEFACTIONS

When Augustus died in AD 14, he had already composed a very full account of what he had achieved, and left orders for it to be posted all over the empire. Its purpose was to show how he 'brought the world under the empire of the Roman people' and it listed 'the private expenses which he devoted to the state and the people'.

These expenses ran to the billions (by today's standards). Augustus listed handouts to every single Roman of 300*ss* in 44 BC (under Julius Caesar's will) and 400*ss* in 29 BC, 24 BC and 11 BC. He bought land for troops in Italy and the provinces to a sum of 860 million *ss*; and gave another 400 million *ss* in 'rewards' to soldiers later on. He transferred private funds of 320 million *ss* to the treasury; he paid for grain distribution among the people when treasury funds ran short; and he built twenty-one temples, restored eighty-five buildings and laid on over eighty games. It is a staggering record. But that is what wealth can do for you – and consider its implications for the economy and the creation of yet more wealth. It also confirmed that the function of the emperor was to serve the interests of the *plebs*. That was a hard-won lesson learned from the collapse of the republic.

AUGUSTUS AND THE *PLEBS*

A certain Vettius had ploughed up a memorial to his father. Augustus remarked: 'That is indeed cultivating your father's memory.'

Macrobius

A CHANGING WORLD

Now that soldiering was not a part-time job as it had been in the republic, the farmer-soldier *pleb* disappeared from the scene. *Plebs* could farm in peace without interruption, or carry on working in towns and cities as artisans, merchants, labourers, shopkeepers, odd-job men and so on, without being called up all the time. They could direct their efforts towards making money and finding a degree of security. The term *plebs* therefore became associated with what we would call a lower class of free citizens, who could make good – though for many of them life would still be something of a struggle.

In other words, in a very wealthy Italy no longer split by almost continual wars between cities, there was the prospect of an economy opening up opportunities for many more people to find work of one sort or another and the gradual emergence of a 'middling class' between the very rich and the destitute.

AUGUSTUS AND THE *PLEBS*

Augustus, hearing of a Roman cavalryman who concealed a debt of 20 million *ss* while he lived, ordered that his pillow be bought for his personal use. There were some raised eyebrows, but he explained: 'The pillow must certainly be conducive to sleep, if that man in spite of all his debts could have slept on it.'

Macrobius

THE EMPEROR AND THE PLEBS

Down in the local baths, the emperor Hadrian (d. AD 138) once saw a veteran of many battles rubbing himself against the wall to get dry, because he could not stretch even to a bit of cloth with which to do the business. 'Have you no slave?' asked the emperor. 'No,' came the reply. The man was immediately given a slave and money. The next day a number of other veterans tried the trick. Hadrian told them to dry each other.

AUGUSTUS AND THE *PLEBS*

Every time Augustus left his residence, a rather scruffy Greek would offer him a complimentary epigram. Augustus rejected it every time, but seeing the Greek approaching again he quickly dashed off an epigram of his own and sent it to him. The Greek read it, praised it, went up to the imperial chair, took a few *asses* out of his purse and gave it to him, saying, 'I swear, Augustus, if I had more, I'd give you more.' Everyone fell about, and Augustus told his steward to pay him a hundred thousand *ss*.

Macrobius

The fact is that, by now, the elite were well aware – none better than the emperor, who knew his ancient history – that they ignored the *plebs* at their peril. The satirical poet Juvenal (d. c. AD 120) may have mocked the *plebs* because they could be kept happy with 'bread and circuses' (i.e. the corn dole and chariot races), but that was not because the *plebs* were lazy or feckless. Far from it. The emperor who laid on shows and ensured a regular grain supply knew that his reign depended on those who had made the empire possible.

And the *plebs* knew it too. They were always prepared to use rough and ready tactics when it came to drawing the attention of the elites to their concerns. Were there food shortages? Time for a street riot – and there were plenty of street leaders happy to organize it.

Political concerns? In a theatre featuring travesties and parodies full of crudity, violence and sex – all wildly popular – the *pleb* audience was in a prime position to make pointed remarks about their political leaders, especially when they knew the leaders were present. Cicero declared that the true feelings of the people were revealed on such occasions, not during political gatherings.

Gladiatorial games and chariot races provided yet more opportunities for the *plebs* to display their feelings. Foolish was the emperor who went to games that he himself had sponsored and did not bother to pay attention, as if contemptuous of them (Julius Caesar was once booed for dealing with his correspondence during the games he had staged). There was always a risk that disorder could break out.

AUGUSTUS AND THE *PLEBS*

Augustus once had reason to complain that some cloth of Tyrian purple which he had ordered was too dark. 'Hold it up higher,' said the tailor, 'and look at it from below.' Augustus replied: 'You mean I've got to walk on the roof before the Roman people can say that I'm well dressed?'

Macrobius

The elites understood this: as the historian Tacitus put it, 'The language of the *plebs* in the circus is not offensive. The place excuses transgression. Ready tolerance of their free speech makes the emperor popular.' And all this put the actual performers themselves in positions of some authority. When it came to financing plays, the emperor would want to hire the very best troupes he could, and that gave the actors leverage with both the emperor and the populace whom they could claim to represent.

So when the emperor entered the amphitheatre or circus to watch the games, he hoped it would be to the cheers of the crowd. But if it was to their curses, he knew he had to up his game.

AUGUSTUS ON THE RECEIVING END

A quip made by a man from one of the provinces is well known. In appearance he closely resembled the emperor, and on his coming to Rome the likeness attracted general attention. Augustus sent for the man and on seeing him said: 'Tell me, young man, was your mother ever in Rome?' 'No,' replied the young man, but could not resist adding, 'But my father was – often.'

Macrobius

APPEALING TO THE EMPEROR

The above quips of Augustus alert us to perhaps the most striking feature of the imperial world: the access that the *plebs* had to the emperor. The *plebs* took pride in their empire and they expected the emperor to take pride in, and listen to, them. There is a famous story about Hadrian, on a tour of the eastern provinces in the AD 120s, hurrying off early in the morning to the local assizes, when he was pulled up by a woman with a problem. He tried to shake her off, telling her he was busy, but her reply was: 'If you're too busy for me, then don't be emperor.' He stopped and listened.

We have accounts of many replies from emperors to local people unsatisfied with the way they had been treated. The reply was often carved in stone and put up in the marketplace of their home city for all to see. Here is an example from the emperor Marcus Aurelius to one Flavia Tertulla:

> We are moved both by the length of time during which, in
> ignorance of the law, you have been married to your uncle,
> and the fact that you were placed in matrimony by your
> grandmother, and by the number of your children. So, as all
> these considerations come together, we confirm that the status
> of your children who resulted from this marriage, which was
> contracted forty years ago, shall be as if they had been conceived
> legitimately.

Two other examples: Hadrian confirmed that women could inherit property from their children, though traditional Roman practice discouraged it. And Severus Alexander declared that landlords could not evict tenants unfairly before their lease expired.

We have sixty-one letters from the provincial governor Pliny the Younger in Bithynia (northern Turkey) to the emperor Trajan, with forty-nine replies — and, at any one time, there could be anything from forty-six to ninety-six governors out there! All of them dealt with pressing issues: *Should I allow a public bath to be built? Should I cover over a drain? What should I do about Christians?* No wonder Seneca (Nero's adviser) wrote: 'So many thousands of people have to be given audience, so many petitions to be dealt with, such a crush of matters coming together from the whole world have to be sorted out, so that it can be submitted in due order to the mind of the most eminent emperor.' The emperor who did not understand his responsibilities in such apparently trivial matters would not last long.

The idea, then, that life for the emperor was one long orgy is far from the truth. He did not have a huge retinue around him and the demands on him were constant, from people like Flavia Tertulla at one end of the scale to the provincial governors whom he had sent out to run the empire. They, too, took a relatively small retinue with them: after all, it was the locals who still ran the show, but under his benign (they hoped) oversight.

AUGUSTUS AND THE *PLEBS*

To a man who was nervously presenting a petition to him, holding out his hand and now withdrawing it, he said: 'Do you think you are giving a present to an elephant?'

Macrobius

POWER AT THE LOCAL LEVEL: POMPEII

But if the *plebs* living in Rome had lost the power of influencing Roman *politics* (p. 193), that was not the case at the local level. After the Social War, Pompeii in 80 BC became a Roman colony doing things the Roman way, with the *plebs* now speaking Latin, not Oscan, and fully involved in local decision-making and also subject to imperial involvement in their affairs.

Pompeii now had a town council, made up of 100 decurions – the wealthy great and good of the town. They were elected every five years and poured their own money into the place, forming a sort of Senate.

Further, every year Pompeians also elected the 'Two Men' – similar to the two consuls – who exercised the judicial and executive power needed to put the decisions of the decurions into action. As in Rome there were also aediles who were in charge of construction, public order, the maintenance of roads, temples and public buildings, and monitoring markets and supplies. Wealth and status qualified Pompeians to stand for election (in Ostia, Rome's port town, your house had to have 1,500 roof tiles for you to qualify!).

EMPEROR CLAUDIUS (D. AD 54): *PLEBS* TO THE RESCUE!

When the area of Rome near the Campus Martius was affected with a rather stubborn fire, and the assistance supplied by the soldiers and his own slaves was not enough, the emperor Claudius had the officials, with chests full of money in front of him, call out the *plebs* from every area of the city, while he urged them to give help by paying each person on the spot a suitable reward for their services.

Suetonius

These positions were fiercely contested, as the election notices painted all over the walls of Pompeii's houses and public buildings make clear. They took certain forms, such as:

Helvius Sabinus, a young man of good character, for aedile.

I ask you to elect as aedile Gnaeus Helvius Sabinus, a young man worthy of every reward, worthy of public office.

Members of the Poppaeus family call for Helvius Sabinus to be made aedile.

It is especially interesting that, while women did not have the vote, there was nothing to stop them supporting the candidates they favoured. Helvius Sabinus was supported by nine women. Among them there was Asellina, who owned a bar, which also provided guest rooms. She had three helpers, Zmyrina, Ismurna and Aegle (one hesitates to guess at the sort of services they provided), who also made their support clear. Taedia, a female member of an important family, supported her grandson!

We have nearly 3,000 examples of such electoral posters. Most were the work of professional sign-writers, and they were almost certainly commissioned by the candidates because the notices cluster along the main streets and around candidates' homes.

EMPEROR NERO (D. AD 65): PRIZES FOR THE *PLEBS*

During a festival period under the emperor Nero, a play called 'The Fire' was put on and the actors were allowed to snatch the furnishings of the burning house and keep them for themselves. Every day, 1,000 birds were released, making a wonderful spectacle, and gifts of all kinds were thrown to the crowds: different sorts of food, tokens to be exchanged for grain, clothes, gold, silver, jewels, pearls, pictures, slaves, working animals, and even tamed wild ones, and finally tokens for ships, blocks of apartments, and farmland.

Suetonius

Note that the posters did not take the form 'Vote for Me', complete with a picture of said candidate, as our election posters do, but 'X asks you to vote for Y'. They often added a descriptor such as 'good man, worthy of public office'.

In other words, it is reputation that counted in the ancient world – and reputation is only what other people can bear witness to. Saying, 'I'm the greatest' is no evidence of anything. Further, these notices highlight the strength of the personal bond between candidate and supporters.

EMPEROR VESPASIAN: THE HEALER (D. JUNE, AD 79)

When Vespasian replaced Nero as emperor, he lacked a
certain dignity and majesty. But he changed all that when
a *pleb* who had lost his sight, and another who was lame,
approached him and begged for the remedy for their ailments
which the god Serapis had revealed in a dream: the emperor
could heal eyes by spitting on them and make whole a leg
if he agreed to touch it with his heel. Vespasian had no
confidence at all that this could possibly succeed and did not
dare put it to the test, but his friends insisted. So in front of a
public assembly he gave it a go and met with success.

Suetonius

BUSINESS INTERESTS

Furthermore, the *plebs* were politically alert. They understood the
advantage of forming themselves into associations to lobby for
the candidate of their choice at election time.

So we find, for example: 'The fruit-pickers ask/urge you to select
X as aedile' or 'All the fishermen say "Elect X as aedile"'. Among
those doing the lobbying were mule-drivers, porters, goldsmiths,
carpenters, cloth-dyers, innkeepers, bakers, barbers, muleteers,
cleaners, millers, chicken-sellers, mat-makers, onion-sellers, apple-
sellers, farmers, grape-pickers and hatters.

Admittedly, there were also the humorists, posting 'The late
drinkers all ask you to vote for Vatia as aedile' – as did 'the sleepers',

'the little thieves', the 'hired assassins' and the 'runaway slaves' – and 'Vote Isidorus for aedile, he licks c… the best'. But that good humour paradoxically indicates how seriously the general population took these notices – seriously enough for some to make fun of them.

THE KINDNESS OF EMPEROR TITUS (D. AD 81)

When Vespasian died, his son Titus took over and immediately earned a reputation as a most kindly ruler. On one occasion, recalling over dinner that he had not given anyone anything during the course of the day, he came out with a memorable comment: 'My friends, I have wasted a day.' Above all, he treated all the *plebs* with such courtesy on every occasion that once, when he announced a gladiatorial show, he declared that he would give it in accordance not with his own wishes but with those of the spectators, and that is exactly what he did.

Indeed, he never denied anything to any petitioners, and of his own accord urged people to ask for what they wanted. Making much of his own enthusiasm for Thracian gladiators, he often engaged with the crowd in lively interchange with words and gestures like a real supporter, but without any loss of dignity or fairness. He omitted nothing that would endear him to the people, frequently attending the baths when the *plebs* were present.

Suetonius

The fact is that the plebs were deeply involved in doing what they could to ensure that their *own* community satisfied their *own* expectations. Nothing could act as more of a spur to doing one's best for oneself and one's family than the sense that those in charge of your community could be trusted to do what you wanted them to, and act in everyone's best interests.

So the *plebs* might no longer have had any direct say in the direction of the Roman state, but they certainly had a regular and active say in the direction of their local community.

FREEDMEN

A slave who had an understanding master – that was crucial (p. 232) – stood a chance of earning his freedom if he gave good service. Freed, he would become a Roman citizen with limited political rights, but his family would be full Roman citizens from then on.

Thousands of freedmen put up inscriptions celebrating such freedom and expressing pride about how it had been achieved. Many became fully engaged in trade, craft, finance (p. 239) and business partnerships, very successfully to judge from the public benefits they bestowed (e.g. staging games) and properties they bought. Though barred from high office, some held local office and some even advised emperors, to the fury of the elites ('dirt and filth', Pliny the Younger called Claudius' Greek advisers, cf. p. 151). They were often looked down upon by Roman citizens (p. 151).

What, then, did everyday life for the *plebs* look like now? Let Pompeii tell its own story.

XI

POMPEII:

AD 79

Pompeii was one of towns that had taken part in the Social War (p. 189). Rome won, and the results of the Roman general Sulla's bombardment can still be seen in Pompeii's pockmarked defensive walls. As we have seen Pompeii became a fully Latin-speaking town (its earlier language had been Oscan, as many inscriptions illustrate, to which Latin was very closely related) and the people of Pompeii became Roman citizens – as did those in almost all the other rebelling cities. They therefore began to take advantage of their new political rights, legal protections and economic opportunities.

The romanization of Pompeii's culture may have been helped initially by Rome's imposition of a settlement of 1,000 retired military veterans, taking over land that had originally belonged to Pompeian rebels. Unwelcome they may have been, but these were not young bloods but grizzled old hands looking forward to settling down and enjoying their retirement. Around 70 BC, they were responsible for sponsoring Pompeii's amphitheatre. Furthermore, these new Roman arrivals began to take over the running of the city from the old families who had traditionally been in charge (p. 195).

As everyone knows, the town was buried by the explosion of Mount Vesuvius in AD 79. The written sources (this is an event very well recorded by Roman historians) agree that it occurred on 24 August AD 79. But archaeologists have analysed the vegetation and theorize that it must have been in the autumn. So what is the answer?

PROBLEM SOLVED BY A HUNGRY PLEB

On that fatal day in AD 79, an unnamed *pleb* had had a very good meal indeed in Pompeii, and celebrated the fact by mentioning it on a graffito he scrawled in charcoal on a street wall. It said: 'On October 17, he was really hungry and gorged himself!' Presumably he had not eaten for some time – or not eaten well, at any rate – and had perhaps just been paid for a job or (as it were) picked up a tenner in the street.

Ah, you will say, but he does not give the year. Obviously, it cannot be after AD 79, but how do we know it was not written in AD 78 or 77? Well, it was written in charcoal on the wall of a street in a busy, bustling town, and a charcoal inscription would not have lasted very long in that location. So 17 October it is – the day of a blowout for a *pleb* before a much bigger one for the whole town.

And this pleb could *write*.

LITERACY

The ancient Roman world has provided us with thousands of official public inscriptions, designed for public consumption. The following was put up in Pompeii by the emperor Vespasian in Latin: 'By the authority of the emperor Caesar Vespasian Augustus: Titus Suedius Clemens, tribune, made an enquiry into public lands seized by private individuals. He carried out a survey and restored them to the Pompeian state.'

Here, then, is the emperor intervening in a local problem, instructing a local tribune to restore stolen state property to its owners, the town of Pompeii (it may have been stolen during the chaos consequent on the demise of Nero, p. 200). Clearly, there would be no point in putting up such notices if the *plebs* were illiterate. All in, about 11,000 graffiti and official notices have been uncovered in Pompeii to date (it may be significant that, when the Roman Empire fell apart in the fifth century AD, there were no more walls covered in graffiti).

Here are just a few from various locations:

Bar: You can get a drink here for only one *as.* You can drink better wine for two *asses.* You can drink best wine for four *asses.*

House: I don't want to sell my husband, not for all the gold in the world.

Launderers' headquarters: Secundus likes to screw boys.

Basilica: Chie, I hope your haemorrhoids rub together so much that they hurt worse than they ever have before!

Herculaneum bar: We pissed on the bed, host. I confess we have done wrong. Why? There was no chamber pot. (Romans had public latrines, served by running water, but few private loos. Those could flood because they had not invented the S- or U-bend.)

Herculaneum house: Apollinaris, the doctor of the emperor Titus, defecated well here.

Entrance hall of a Pompeian house (part of a seven-day list, like the week's shopping list, though the Roman week lasted eight days; priced in asses): (Day 1) bread VIII, oil III, wine III; (2) bread VIII, oil V, onion V, cooking pot I, bread for slaves II, wine II; (3) bread VIII, bread for slave IV, porridge III, etc. The list also included wheat, beef, dates, incense, cheese, sausage, whitebait and leeks.

We also have graffiti written by children practising the alphabet (the letters in almost exactly the same order as they are in our alphabet and also in the original Phoenician version [p. 163]) and drawing cartoons, one picturing the maze in which the Minotaur was kept. It was headed *LABYRINTHUS HIC HABITAT MINOTAURUS* ('Labyrinth here lives Minotaur' – difficult language, Latin).

None of these would have appeared if only a few people could read and write – and that emphasizes a very important point indeed. Reading, writing and arithmetic are absolutely essential for driving business and developing a flourishing economy. One cannot do business without contracts, bills, wills, advertisements, loan agreements, laws, guarantees and so on. Pompeii provides myriad examples.

LOCATION, LOCATION

Pompeii is fifteen miles south of Naples. Its town walls, complete with towers and seven or eight gates, enclose an area of about 160 acres (around half the size of Hyde Park in London), of which two-thirds have been excavated. Its population is much debated: the baseline is about 10,000–20,000, although some estimates even raise it to 40,000.

It is located in the phenomenally fertile area of Campania. As the ancient author Florus put it: 'Nothing is more temperate than its climate – indeed its spring flowers blossom twice; nothing is more fertile; there is said to be a competition between grape and wheat growers; nothing is more welcoming than its sea, its harbours and its springs.' It was a place where agriculture flourished.

Even better (and less well known), it was a port town located at the mouth of the Sarno river (some think there may have been two harbours, but there is no certainty about where they might have been located). This made Pompeii a trading hub, serving many of the inland towns in the region, like Nuceria and Nola. That enabled them (at a price) to both receive goods from and ship goods to Naples and the much larger port of Puteoli, and from there on to Rome and elsewhere. From Pompeii local products such as wine, olive oil, wool, fish sauce (*garum*), salt, walnuts, figs, spices, and even slaves were shipped throughout the Mediterranean and beyond (wine amphoras from Pompeii have been found in Middlesex). Wine production, it has been calculated, was four times greater than the region itself required. That resulted in a flourishing export trade, and Vesuvian wine was found in Italy, Germany, Spain and Africa.

GARUM

One speciality of Pompeii was the popular fish sauce called *garum* or *liquamen*. It was made by rotting down salted fish for two months under a blazing sun – the innards of mackerel and tunny fish were the preferred ingredients – until it was liquid and served as such, or with a variety of different spices. It was a culinary ingredient, and was used to enhance foods of many sorts, including sweets. It has been likened to modern South-East Asian fish sauce.

The star producer in Pompeii was Aulus Umbricius Scaurus, who produced *garum* in various grades and exported it as well (it has been found in France). 'The best *liquamen*, from the shop of Scaurus,' he boasted on some of his amphoras. He ran at least seven shops in Pompeii and was a political figure too; a statue of him was even set up in the Forum. He became extremely wealthy and owned a fabulous villa overlooking the harbour, featuring a large mosaic floor decorated with – you guessed it – amphoras of his own products, on which his own name featured large.

Pompeii's wide regional connections were economically very significant, creating plenty of opportunity for mutual trade between towns, and plenty of work for the *plebs*: filling in the paperwork relating to that trade and transporting its goods by draught-animal wagons from place to place, loading and unloading ships, and so on. (It has been calculated that unloading all the vessels at Ostia in Rome would have required about 25,000 single 'carries' a day – work for a good few men.)

These facilities and Pompeii's agricultural fertility enabled trade to flourish, raising the revenues to both provide the *plebs* with work and maintain the elite lifestyles typical of the Roman great and good, who betook themselves into this region south of Naples during the hot summer months to escape from the sweltering, smoky, mosquito-ridden city. They all owned lavish villas here and looked to the local *plebs* to provide the expensive goods and services that they demanded while they networked with each other and with the local Greek intellectuals they so admired.

The basic point is that the more trade and business there was, the more traders would be attracted, the wealthier the area would become, the more work would be available for the locals, and the higher the general standard of living would rise.

MAKING A LIVING

To the people of Pompeii, commerce and profit were hugely respected and desired: Mercury, the god of commerce, was worshipped and often displayed outside shops, on walls and on sales counters. Numerous inscriptions were found that emphasized the importance of profit: 'Welcome, profit!' 'Profit is joy!'

We hear of many ways for a Pompeian *pleb* to have earned a living: apple-seller, baker, banker, barber, bath attendant, builder, carpenter, carriage-driver, chicken-keeper, clapper-beater, cleaner, cloak-seller, cobbler, cushion-seller, doorman, dyer, engraver, farmer, felt-worker, fisherman, fruit-seller, fuller, furnace-stoker, gem-cutter, goldsmith, grape-picker, guard, hatter, herdsman, innkeeper, lupin-seller, mat-maker, miller, moneylender, mule driver, ointment-seller, onion-seller, outfitter, painter, pastry-cook, pig-breeder, porter, priest's attendant, prostitute, rag-and-bone man, sauce-maker, scorer, scribe, soothsayer, spinner, surveyor, tanner, theatre official, waggoner, weaver, wine-seller, wool-worker.

One (Roman) graffito jokes about multi-tasking: 'You've had eight different job opportunities – barman, clay-worker, dealer in salted fish, baker, farmer, maker of bronze trinkets, retailer and now dealer in jugs. Just lick c---- and you'll have done the lot.'

HONEST MERCHANTS

The problem facing merchants selling goods in quantities was that the *plebs* often suspected that they were being cheated. Today, we have no problems about people earning a reasonable 'profit'. But that could be suspect in the ancient world, probably because bartering still went on among the poor, and 'profit' did not come into the equation as it did with money, because money can be spent on anything. Bartering – changing stuff for stuff – just left you with... stuff. The result was that merchants tended to work together in groups, taking advantage of the *collegia* system to develop a public reputation for honest dealing (there are records of penalties for bad behaviour). When St Paul, who was a tent-maker, arrived in Athens, he joined up with a network of established tent-makers. As Publilius Syrus (d. 43 BC) put it, 'The man of whom all speak well will receive the favours of the people.'

Funerary monuments are a rich source of evidence for occupa-tions. Quite apart from political and military roles, we hear of architects, auctioneers, pearl merchants, cattle merchants, doctors, bedchamber-slaves, clerks, accountants, public slaves, stone-sawyers and innkeepers. A clown was memorialized as follows: 'Here is laid the jolly old clown Protogenes, slave of Clulius, who made many and many a delight for people by his fooling.'

COLLEGIA

Elite Romans were always suspicious of gatherings of ordinary people behind closed doors, on the grounds that they might foment trouble (p. 70). Nevertheless, from early times, *collegia* had been allowed to develop (cf. Numa, p. 32, if Livy is to be believed). Many of these were friendly associations. Their main purpose was to foster goodwill among members, who included both *plebs* and slaves.

Many also acted as dining clubs and/or burial clubs, ensuring that members were bid farewell with all due ceremonial and their memory preserved: they each had their name and job inscribed on a burial urn kept in the club headquarters. And many of these monuments reflect their great pride in their skills and their achievements. The titles of over 250 occupations are recorded in this way from the city of Rome alone – everything from a maker of balustrades to a maker of eyes for statues and a plucker of body hair.

Collegia also attracted wealthy senators as patrons, who could benefit politically from the connection. Some were set up to serve those with business or political interests. It may be that those groups mentioned above, urging citizens to vote for certain candidates for office, were of the latter sort.

SHOPS IN POMPEII

There were about 600 shops in all, of which 35 were bakeries and about 150 were bars and inns serving hot food and wine, in which our *pleb* who solved the dating problem (p. 216) could have had his blowout. Graffiti in these bars show the *plebs* drinking, gaming and fighting. Given that many *plebs* lived in dark, one-room wooden garrets or lean-to shacks against a convenient wall where it would be unwise to light a fire, it is not surprising that poorer Pompeiians would bring their food to be cooked there.

Some bars also functioned as grocery shops: the counters usually had large clay jars embedded in them, probably holding grains, dried fruits, vegetables and so on; wine was kept in clay amphoras, many of which have survived. One bar featured a list of products that it had ordered for customers, informing us on what days they were purchased and how many were bought. We read of cuts of meat 'fetched smoking hot from wayside cookshops', tripe, green vegetables, dried beans, and 'hot tarts' on the menu. Children accompanied their parents to the shops. We find stick-men and stick-gladiators scratched or drawn, low down beneath the counters, clearly by children accompanying an adult.

What other shops sold is often impossible to tell because the evidence was lost in the destruction of the town. But a wall painting shows a man displaying shoes, cloth merchants showing samples to two women, a man hammering a metal vessel, another selling bread, and a fruit and vegetable stall. Pompeii's town square featured fixed locations for the fish, meat and vegetable markets. The sign on one shop at least indicates that it was a coppersmith's.

Plenty of regular work there.

A JOKE

An ill-tempered man was playing a game, when an idle man sat down beside him and started chatting. Crossly, the former asked him, 'What's your work? Or do you just laze about?' 'I mend clothes, but I don't have any work,' came the reply. 'Here, mend this then and shut up!' the first man replied, ripping his tunic and handing it to him.

FEATURES OF POMPEIAN LIFE

It is not surprising that, in a country with the climate of Italy, it was much better to be outside than inside, especially if 'inside' was as unappealing as the sort of accommodation that was available to the poor. And if you were outside, it is very likely you would want to drop into places where your friends were, probably having a drink.

Of course, the elite came to despise what they saw as the 'workless' plebs hanging about in the squares, the bars, the temples, and in the barbers and the public lavatories, arguing, gambling, discussing the gladiators, the chariot drivers, the actors, the prostitutes, the politicians whom they did – or did not – admire, and, for those who made it their career, their military experiences. The nature of that particular camaraderie is well known: at this time, the now professionalized (under Augustus, p. 199) Roman army was spending long periods abroad and must have come back with many fine tales to tell of life in distant lands. But the *plebs* in the bars did not give a fig for what the elite thought about them.

THE *PLEBS* AND THE ELITE

Between themselves, the elite usually had it in for the *plebs*. Descriptions such as *promisca* (indiscriminate), *fanatica* (fanatical), *perdita* (depraved), *sordida* (filthy), *faex* (scum), *infima* (despicable), *inops vulgus* (destitute mob), *vulgus imperitum* (ignorant mob) and *vulgus impudens vel imprudens* (foolish and shameless mob) were common. Nothing surprising about that ...

GAMBLING

Gambling was enormously popular. When the weather was too bad to work, what else was there for the *plebs* to do? Children often left school to enjoy a quick bet. Gaming tables could be found scratched into pavements all over the place, especially in barracks and even more so in bars. One witness of the Roman sack of Corinth in 146 BC (p. 179) said that he saw soldiers scratching gaming tables on magnificent works of art.

But the *plebs* were simply imitating the emperors. Augustus loved gambling; when Nero gambled, the minimum stake was

400,000*ss*; Claudius wrote a book about it and even had a gaming
board fixed inside his carriage so that he could gamble as he was
carried from place to place.

There was no organized betting industry as there is nowadays.
The *plebs* could bet only among themselves, at the gladiatorial games
and the racing – and even while being taken off for execution, as
did the Stoic philosopher Canus (d. c. AD 39). He asked the soldier
escorting him to take note that he was one point ahead in the game,
in case his opponent claimed he had won.

'Hunting, bathing, gaming, laughing – that's living' went the
saying. Dying, too, it appears.

A PHILOSOPHICAL BAR

In a tavern in Ostia, the seaport of ancient Rome, wall
paintings from about the year AD 100 depict ordinary men
sitting on the bench toilets of a public latrine. Painted
above them are seven sages in scholarly dress, seated on
thrones. Associated with each sage is ironic text providing
wisdom on the men's immediate concern, e.g.:

Solon of Athens: 'To shit well, Solon rubbed his belly.'

Thales of Miletus: 'Thales admonished those shitting to
strain hard.'

Chilon of Lacedaemon: 'Cunning Chilon taught to fart
silently.'

The three named men were ancients long dead and
famous for their wise sayings, but they must have been
well-known even among the *plebs*, otherwise their 'wisdom'

would not have raised a laugh. Today we might replace them with, ooh, let's see now, Piers Morgan, Sir Stephen Fry...

ATTRACTING BUSINESS

Since all work and no play makes Jack a dull boy, Pompeii provided plenty of entertainment to draw in locals, businesses, and visitors from surrounding areas and beyond. Mention has already been made of the amphitheatre, sponsored by retired veterans (p. 215). It held 15,000–20,000 spectators ready to enjoy gladiators, boxers, wild beast hunts and much more.

POST-MATCH PUNCH-UP

The Roman historian Tacitus saw fit to record the details of serious disorder in AD 59 between Pompeii's gladiatorial squad and the away team from Nuceria:

> There was an exchange of abuse – typical of these unruly provincial towns – which led to stone throwing and drawn swords. The Pompeians came off best. Very many of the Nucerians were wounded or mutilated and taken to Rome, and many parents and children lamented their loss. The emperor ordered the Senate to investigate the affair, who passed it on to the consuls. When they reported back to the Senate, Pompeii was forbidden to stage any such events again for ten years. The sponsors of the event and the instigators of the disorder were exiled.

Pompeii's Grand Theatre could seat 5,000 people and hosted mime, acting, juggling and musical performances. The smaller Odeon was used for concerts, lectures, and poetry readings. A gymnasium and exercise ground (*palaestra*) were available, in which males young and old could run, throw the discus, wrestle and swim.

THE BROTHEL

It was once thought that Pompeii must have had an unfeasibly large number of brothels, simply because the bars that offered accommodation were often found to have sexual graffiti scrawled on the bedroom walls. But as far as we know, there was only one official brothel in the town. The explicit, numbered illustrations in the entrance, perhaps demonstrating the wide range of the possibilities on offer, must have satisfied most tastes ('I'd like number three, please, with a touch of number six and perhaps a hint of four').

STEPHANUS' LAUNDRY

The great and the good must look smartly dressed, especially after travelling a long way. Stephanus, one of the four large launderers in Pompeii (there were also smaller ones), provided the full range of services in this noble cause:

- Treading basins containing urine – there was a public urinal directly outside – and fuller's earth (a special form of clay) to get the grease out (camel's urine was highly prized).

- Washing and rinsing basins (with a water supply).

- A drying area on a balcony.

- A pressing area.

A skeleton was excavated in the doorway, with 1089ss scattered about him in assorted coins – perhaps Stephanus himself trying to escape the eruption?

There were also six dye-shops in Pompeii. Orange, red, yellow, indigo blue, purple, black, brown, grey and green dyes may all have been available.

THE BATHS

And that there were baths – a Roman's favourite leisure centre – goes without saying. Pompeii had four bath complexes (one outside the city walls) to serve its population and visitors. The most interesting one is the Stabian complex. This is the earliest Roman bath we know of. It was built in the fourth century BC in the style of Greek baths: small chambers, each containing a hip bath, fed by a well.

HIP BATHS

It was a hip bath that enabled the ancient Greek Archimedes to discover his famous 'flotation' principle: that the volume of an object – in this case, his body – is equal to the volume of water it displaces. Presumably he stood up and sat down again and again in the hip bath, noticing how much water he spilled out each time. He could hardly have noticed any difference to the water level after getting in and out of a huge swimming pool!

But the Stabian complex was reworked and extended over the years to include female baths, a wrestling area, and an actual *swimming* pool (some others even had lecture halls, discussion groups, sports areas and libraries!). A major development took place in c. 80 BC, when it was fitted with a hypocaust (underfloor heating). One side of the complex was flanked by shops.

Baths were not usually for swimming in. They were for exercising, chatting and relaxing in, moving from cold baths to warm baths, hot baths, sweating rooms, and finally a cleansing room where you scraped off the oil and sweat with a metal instrument called a strigil. It was usual for the elite to invite their friends to the baths rather than, as we might do, to a bar, before inviting them back to the house for dinner. Wealthy Romans even had private bath complexes in their villas. One has been found in Pompeii.

LIMELIGHT ON CONCRETE

The ancients knew all about burning limestone to create quicklime, which, mixed with water, sand or rubble, produced mortar. But it took a long time to dry and would not dry underwater.

In the second century BC, some Roman mixed lime with pink volcanic ash. This, containing alumina and silica, created a very strong and durable concrete that could be poured into moulds and even set underwater. It revolutionized Roman building techniques and was used in the construction of Pompeii's baths.

Romans loved their baths. Indeed, supplying them was one of the main purposes of building aqueducts. Rome, for example, eventually had eleven aqueducts, 300 miles' worth in all, providing about 250 million gallons of water a day for the million inhabitants! It supplied drinking water, of course, but also fountains, water features, public latrines (p. 217) and flowers across the city – but mainly the baths.

But while everyone, *plebs* and the elite alike, used the baths, it was clear who was who: the poor *pleb*, with a single thin towel (p. 204); the wealthy arriving with their slaves, fine clothes and jewellery, departing well-oiled and perfumed.

SLAVES

Buying a slave was an investment: they were expensive to purchase – an educated one very expensive indeed – and expensive to maintain, as they needed board, lodging and medical care. They were also part of everyday life. Everyone knew that it was in the master's interests to look after his slaves, and it was in the slave's interests to cooperate. If slaves won their master's approval, they could be freed, and they and their family from then on would be Roman citizens. A bad master or an uncooperative slave meant endless trouble for everyone. Seneca (d. AD 65), adviser to the emperor Nero, said that owners who mistreated their slaves were despised.

It is important to point out that slaves were bought to fill precisely the same range of jobs as were done by the *plebs*. In other words, they were bought because people *needed* anyone from a washer-upper, farm labourer, builder, nurse, teacher or cook, to an actor, dancer, musician or gymnast, to an architect, financial accountant or top civil servant. Since slaves looked the same as everyone else and no occupations were reserved exclusively for them, they mixed unnoticed among the *plebs*.

The point here is that a slave was a human resource. You wanted them to be useful to you. The skills they possessed were very important, and, if they were interested in learning other ones, all to the good. They could, for example, be sent to a master craftsman to learn a business. There would have been plenty of highly skilled slaves – some bought for that purpose, others trained up – working cooperatively alongside the *pleb* artisans in Pompeii, all quite normally, and enjoying the same public services as everyone else (p. 55).

And all this raises the question: would you rather be a slave or a down-and-out, sheltering at night among the tombs of the dead? There is no doubt that for some slavery was a lifeline (p. 214, 238–9), for others (e.g. those sent down the mines) a death sentence.

OUTNUMBERED!

The philosopher Seneca tells of a proposal once made in the Senate that slaves should be made easily recognizable by having to wear distinctive clothing. 'It then became apparent what a dangerous threat we would face if our slaves began to realize how few we were!'

HIGH-END WORK: ARTS AND CRAFTS

The Roman statesman and philosopher Cicero (d. 44 BC) was one of the many elites who were contemptuous of the *plebs*, at least when they turned into what he saw as uncontrollable and brainless political mobs (i.e. when they didn't agree with him). He was also known to cast aspersions on mere workmen. Nevertheless, he did acknowledge the skills that they possessed. On one occasion he wrote:

> Consider how useful are the hands which nature has given to man, and how fit for exercising all sorts of skills! With their help, the hand can paint, carve, engrave, play stringed instruments and the pipe. These supply us with recreation, but also with necessities: tilling the ground, building houses, weaving or sewing garments, and working in brass and iron... it is the hand that executes, and to the hands that we owe our buildings, clothes, a secure life, our cities, walls, homes and temples...
>
> We discover the hidden veins of copper, silver, and gold, for practical purposes and for our adornment. We cut down trees, and use every kind of wild and cultivated timber, not only to make fire to warm us and cook our food, but also for building, so that we have houses to protect us from the heat and cold. With timber we build ships, which bring us everything we need for living from all over the world...

Cicero's letters frequently discuss the ways in which he wanted his various villas decorated with superb Greek-style artefacts

– or the real thing. He might well have ordered some from Pompeii.

THE HOMES OF THE WEALTHY

Anyone who has been to Pompeii will know how magnificently the houses of the wealthy were decorated with Greek-style architectural features (temples, basilicas, etc.), frescoes (artwork produced by paint applied to wet plaster, to seal and secure it) and so on.

These highly coloured murals and mosaics are among the Roman world's best-preserved works of art, showing fabulous scenes from myth (gods, goddesses, heroes and heroines), everyday life, landscapes, animals, fish and even architectural features, rather as if someone wanted their lounge to look like St Paul's Cathedral or Trafalgar Square. Many clients had their walls decorated with windowpanes, doors, architectural features, and even buildings.

No less impressive is the huge range of artefacts that have been recovered. Of course, there was no lack of implements for everyday work and military use: farming tools, kitchenware, swords, spears, shields and so on. What is impressive is the sheer range of pottery, lamps, cooking utensils, furniture (bed frames, chairs, tables), glassware (mirrors, decanters, cups), amphoras used for storing wine and olive oil, and metalwork. Jewellery and personal items included rings, necklaces, bracelets, combs, cosmetic instruments and ceramics. In one small house a wooden chest was discovered containing 140 precious stones and glass paste beads, some fully worked, some partially cut, together with gem-cutting tools.

Superb statuary features humans, animals, hunting scenes, gods, heroes and heroines.

None of this happened by accident. It came about because of the *demand* for it and this resulted in a form of 'mass production' of murals from painters' workshops in the town, each working on its own specialities, to satisfy as many clients as possible – from the elite to the better-off *plebs*. Mural painting was a huge business, involving large teams of highly skilled slaves and *plebs*, all with their own particular skills. Further, while the seriously wealthy were the main consumers of such items, the next 25 per cent or so were also able to enjoy peristyles (rectangular gardens surrounded by pillars and colonnades) and 'panel pictures' showing scenes from mythology.

The same can be said of the artefacts. Locally produced or imported, they ranged from the fabulously expensive to the relatively cheap, all produced by highly skilled *pleb* and slave artisans serving as wide a range of the public as possible.

Pompeii, then, at one end of the scale, was 'embedded in regional and super-regional trade networks', as one scholar put it, meeting the demands of the Roman imperial elite, who knew exactly what they wanted their summer villas to look like. But it is clear that there was an associated trickle-down effect, of which even moderately well-off Pompeians could take full advantage.

Further, the labour required for supplying and supporting such businesses must have been very significant.

RELATIVE VALUES IN THE FOURTH CENTURY AD

To get some idea of the relative value of work – farm labourers, mule drivers, sewer cleaners, shepherds and other general labour could earn 100*ss* per day. Skilled labourers earned much more: carpenters and stone masons 200*ss*, wall mosaic workers 240*ss*, wall painters 300*ss*, and figure painters 600*ss*.

STANDARD OF LIVING

It seems that a remarkably varied diet was available to the *plebs* in this part of Italy. A tunnel ran under an apartment block in the neighbouring town of Herculaneum, fed by chutes from the kitchens and waste products of the 150 inhabitants above. The waste has survived because the sewer did not drain properly – it was blocked by volcanic deposit in the eruption of Vesuvius. The composted human waste has been found to contain a wide range of foods including emmer, millet, barley, lentils, apples, pears, dill, fennel, poppy seed, *garum*, walnuts, anchovies, sea bream, damsel-fish and horse mackerel (114 different foodstuffs in all). Sugar was known, but rarely used, and then only as a medicine.

Further, as archaeological work informs us, Pompeiians could choose from local or provincially produced wine, olive oil, fish sauce, and over fourteen different types of fruit including apples, pears, plums, peaches, blackberries, cherries, walnuts and pine nuts; dates and black pepper were imported. Emmer wheat and millet grew well there, as did lentils and broad beans, figs, onions and cabbages.

So city life in a pretty average block of flats was not all vegetables and porridge: even among low and middling *pleb* families there was considerable dietary diversity to be enjoyed (and perhaps prices were driven down by such diversity). The skeletal remains of the AD 79 eruption demonstrate that a surprising number of victims seem to have been pretty robust, many living to a good old age (there is little evidence of age-related disorders in the bones). Whatever problems Pompeians had, diet does not seem to have been one of them.

MILLIONAIRE SLAVES

Trade was a 'dirty' business that the elite would not touch with a bargepole – or that is what they said after being prevented from engaging with it long ago (p. 168). But since it could make them vast sums of money, they put the bargepole into the hands of their slaves. Not that slaves (let alone women!) could legally engage in such business, let alone own anything, but in this case it became so common that, as Roman jurists tell us, 'the law turned a blind eye'. Slaves therefore became involved on behalf of their masters – though not instructed by them; that would make the master responsible if things went wrong – in commercial enterprises great and small, from mercantile and marine operations, financial transactions and tax collecting to banking and real estate. They shared in the profits with their masters, and took the money when freed.

Women likewise could go into business, run banks, work as doctors, advocates, accountants, traders and so on. It would take 1,000 years before women in Europe had such power again. No wonder some free Romans agreed to become slaves for a fixed period.

FINANCE

Commerce is, of course, a main driver of wealth. But so too is the capacity to borrow money in order to expand one's business. That comes from banking services, which in the Roman world meant private financial businesses ready to lend money. The following is an example of the archives that survive on wax wooden tablets describing such financial transactions.

Gaius needs money and borrows it in the shape of loans, transacted through the good offices of one Hesychus, a slave, guaranteed against large quantities of wheat and vegetables, all located in a named stall in Puteoli, thirty miles from Pompeii:

Copy of documents: Gaius, for receiving loans of HS [sesterces] 3,000, in addition to the other HS 10,000, against a pledge of wheat. [Date] I, Gaius wrote that I received as loans from and owe to Hesychus, the sum of HS 3,000 in cash, in addition to the other HS 10,000 in cash which by another document of mine I shall pay to him. Hesychus stipulated that he be duly paid in good coin the HS 3,000 written above; I, Gaius, solemnly promised to do so. I gave him as a pledge for the whole sum 60,000 litres of Alexandrian wheat, which is placed in the Public Granaries in Puteoli, on the middle level in grain stall 12, and 200 sacks of lentils, chickpeas, and flour, which hold 35,000 litres, which are placed in the same grain-stalls, and which I store at my entire risk against all danger [e.g. fire, rot, etc.].

The more commercially-minded people there were who had the confidence to borrow against their assets in order to develop their business in the context of a relatively stable society, the better the chance of raising general living standards. The wealth generated by the Roman Empire encouraged this to happen across increasing sectors of society.

That was the Augustan revolution in action in one small town in Italy. It was probably replicated over much of the empire, in the sense of a massive disparity between the very rich and hideously poor but also of opportunity for those with the desire and ability to seize it – because if you did not, someone else would. Here is the famous Maktar inscription from Numidia, a far-flung part of the Roman empire in the Tunisia-Algeria region, c. AD 270. It tells its own story, a very different one from that of the peasant Simylus with which our story began:

I was born in poverty. My father was poor and we had no property or house of our own. From birth I have lived by working the land. The land has had no rest and nor have I.

When the harvest ripened, I was the first to reap it. When gangs of harvesters arrived in the fields, I was still the first to harvest mine ahead of everyone else, piling up the sheaves behind my back, as I did for others too under the blazing sun, more than anyone else.

I did this for twelve years and as a result I was made foreman and managed teams of harvesters, cutting the fields of Numidia. All this hard work and my refusal to be content with little, eventually brought me an expensive home and farmstead.

It also brought me the rewards of office. I am a senator in the city, I took my seat in the Senate house, and this poor farm boy actually became censor. I have watched my children and grandchildren grow up around me. In line with our merits, we have enjoyed years of fame, without any malevolent accusations.

Mortals, learn to lead blameless lives. The one who has lived blamelessly deserves to die blamelessly.

LAST WORDS: THE IMPORTANCE OF THE PLEBS

When the Roman republic (*res publica*) was threatening to collapse about him in the late 50s BC, the Roman statesman Cicero wrote a dialogue, *On the Republic*. In it, he reflected what *res publica* (literally, 'public affairs, business, property') actually meant. He defined its essence as '*people* coming together to form a society by agreeing about what justice is and mutually participating in its advantages'.

Such a society could not but be a *res populi* – 'a matter of interest [actually] *belonging to/in the charge of* the people'. But if those matters were taken over by, and so in charge of, a tyrant (i.e. Julius Caesar, whom Cicero at the time greatly feared), the people would lose those rights of 'justice' and 'mutual advantage' that lay at the heart of a free republic and gave the *populus* their *libertas*.

Cicero then gave a historical account of how the Roman 'constitution' in fact relied on *trust*: the people entrusting (not transferring) their rights first to kings, and later to a Senate consisting of those leaders (consuls, etc.) whom the people had themselves elected. Rome's success sprang from the *fides* ('good faith, trustworthiness') of its leaders in respecting the rights entrusted to them. Elsewhere Cicero used an image from guardianship to make the same point: 'management of the *res publica* should be conducted in the interests of those entrusted to one's care, and not of those to whom the management has been entrusted'; and further on, 'every leader should understand that he represents the city and ought to maintain its dignity and distinction, preserve its laws, dispense justice and remember what has been entrusted to his good faith'.

Those 'republican principles' found their origins in the great 'conflict of the orders' between the *plebs* and the patricians, and have been worked and reworked in the more than two and a half millennia since: from Menenius Agrippa's speech to the *plebs* in 494 BC (p. 72), Cicero and Seneca, through the Renaissance, Machiavelli (d. 1527), Hobbes (d. 1679), Montesquieu (d. 1755) and, admittedly indirectly, Rousseau's (d. 1778) definitive analysis of class conflict and the origins of social inequality, to the modern day.

The 'democratic' turns of the nineteenth and twentieth centuries, in relation to the Roman ideas of workers' power, the codification of laws (the Twelve Tables, p. 99), and the empowerment of popular assemblies, have been especially influential.

The Roman *plebs*, then, were at the very start of the thinking that has emerged as what we mean by the republican principles behind modern 'democracy', i.e. that we the people possess the right, under the law, to:

1. run our own affairs;

2. outsource that running to elected office-holders with a mandate to serve our interests and not theirs; and

3. vote them in and out of office.

We in the West are extraordinarily fortunate to live in societies whose government is organized around principles so simple, but so fundamental to human freedom and happiness, which the Roman *plebs* played such a crucial role in establishing.

BIBLIOGRAPHY

Balsdon, J. P. V. D., *Life and Leisure in Ancient Rome* (Bodley Head, 1969)

Beard, M., *S.P.Q.R.* (Profile, 2015)

Berry, J., *The Complete Pompeii* (Thames and Hudson, 2007)

Bettenson, H. (trans.), *Livy: Rome and the Mediterranean* (Penguin Classics, 1976)

Bond, S. E., *Strike: Labor, Unions, and Resistance in the Roman Empire* (Yale University Press, 2025)

Bradley, K., and Cartledge, P. (eds), *The Cambridge World History of Slavery (vol. 1): The Ancient Mediterranean World* (Cambridge University Press, 2011)

Campbell, B., *The Romans and their World: A Short Introduction* (Yale University Press, 2011)

Cooley, A. E., and Cooley, M. G. L., *Pompeii: A Sourcebook* (Routledge, 2004)

Cornell, T. J., *The Beginnings of Rome* (Routledge, 1995)

Dalby, A., *Food in the Ancient World from A–Z* (Routledge, 2003)

de Sélincourt, A. (trans.), *Livy: The War with Hannibal* (Penguin Classics, 1965)

de Sélincourt, A. (trans.), *Livy: The Early History of Rome* (Penguin Classics, 1960)

Flohr, M., and Wilson, A. (eds), *The Economy of Pompeii* (Oxford University Press, 2017)

Frayn, J. M., *Subsistence Farming in Roman Italy* (Centaur Press, 1979)

Grig, L., *Popular Culture in the Ancient World* (Cambridge University Press, 2017)

Horsfall, N., *The Culture of the Roman Plebs* (Duckworth, 2003)

Jones, P., and Sidwell, K., *The World of Rome* (Cambridge University Press, 1997)

Jones, P., *Veni, Vidi, Vici: Everything You Ever Wanted to Know About the Romans But Were Afraid to Ask* (Atlantic, 2013)

Knapp, P., *Invisible Romans* (Profile, 2011)

Lomas, K., *The Rise of Rome* (Profile, 2017)

Luce, T. J. (trans.), *Livy: The Rise of Rome, Books One to Five* (Oxford World's Classics, 1998)

Milner, N. P., *Vegetius: Epitome of Military Science* (Liverpool University Press, 1993)

Morgan, T., *Popular Morality in the Roman Empire* (Cambridge University Press, 2007)

Oakley, S. P., *A Commentary on Livy, Books VI–X* (Oxford University Press, 1998)

Ogilvie, R., *A Commentary on Livy, Books I–V* (Oxford University Press, 1965)

Radice, B. (trans.), *Livy: Rome and Italy, Books VI–X* (Penguin Classics, 1982)

Sancinito, J., *The Reputation of the Roman Merchant* (Michigan University Press, 2024)

Scott-Kilvert, I. (trans.), *Polybius: The Rise of the Roman Empire* (Penguin Classics, 1979)

Shipley, G., and Salmon, J., *Human Landscapes in Classical Antiquity* (Routledge, 1996)

Toner, J., *Leisure and Ancient Rome* (Polity, 1995)

Toner, J., *Popular Culture in Ancient Rome* (Polity, 2009)

Verboven, K., and Laes, C., *Work, Labour, and Professions in the Roman World* (Brill, 2016)

Wallace-Hadrill, A., *Rome's Cultural Revolution* (Cambridge University Press, 2008)

White, K. D., *Country Life in Classical Times* (Elek, 1977)

Yardley, J. C. (trans.), *Livy: Rome's Italian Wars Books VI–X* (Oxford World's Classics, 2013)

Yardley, J. C. (trans.), *Livy: The Dawn of the Roman Empire Books 31–40* (Oxford World's Classics, 2000)

ACKNOWLEDGEMENTS

My thanks to Ed Faulkner (Atlantic Books) for proposing this topic, which it has been a great pleasure to investigate.

I am extremely grateful, as ever, to Jeannie Cohen, with whom I have been privileged to work for many years on many classical projects and who has, as ever, put me straight on so much that I have written.

Peter Jones
July 2025

INDEX